HOW TO BE A SUPERNATURAL LOVER

Also by Sherron Mayes

Be Your Own Psychic

HOW TO BE A SUPERNATURAL LOVER

TUNING IN YOUR PSYCHIC POWERS FOR YOUR BEST EVER RELATIONSHIP

SHERRON MAYES

HODDER

MOBIUS

First published in Great Britain in 2003 by Hodder and Stoughton
A division of Hodder Headline

A Mobius Book

1 3 5 7 9 10 8 6 4 2

ISBN 0 340 73460 4

Typeset in Adobe Caslon, StampGothic and Meta by
Phoenix Typesetting, Burley-in-Wharfedale, West Yorkshire

Printed and bound in Great Britain by Clays Ltd, St Ives plc

Hodder and Stoughton
A division of Hodder Headline
338 Euston Road
London NW1 3BH

Dedicated to everyone who believes in love

'You know that place between sleep and awake,
the place where you can still remember dreaming?
That's where I'll always love you Peter Pan.
That's where I'll be waiting.'

Tinkerbell, from *Peter Pan*

ACKNOWLEDGEMENTS

With thanks to Rowena Webb for having faith in my idea and to my editor Emma Heyworth-Dunn for her eye for detail and helping me to clarify my thoughts and insights.

CONTENTS

YOUR PSYCHIC FORMULA FOR LOVE

1

DISCOVER YOUR HIDDEN POTENTIAL TO TRANSFORM YOUR RELATIONSHIPS

The moment you have in your heart this extraordinary thing called love
And feel the depth, the delight, the ecstasy of it,
you will discover that for you the world is transformed.
J. KRISHNAMURTI, 1895–1986, SAGE AND PHILOSOPHER

Since time began, everyone has, at some time in their lives, pondered over some puzzling mysteries: why is it that we feel magnetically drawn to certain people and what is that magical energy called 'love' that's evoked from such meetings?

Strong attraction is a powerful force that can mean different things to us. We all have memories of when just a few words or even a glance have been the catalyst for a lovesick crush or, perhaps more mysteriously, when someone we disliked could render us helpless with emotion. Such enigmas are what make the topic of love so fascinating and at times bewildering.

In my own life, I have been amazed by the many types of 'connections' I have experienced. How could meeting a man for the first time send my temperature soaring and make my heart race with passion? Or why could I talk to someone new and feel as if I had known them for years? What intrigued me even more about these encounters was the undeniable psychic energy between us that, at times produced a powerful telepathy – and yet this immense potential couldn't ensure a long-lasting, loving relationship. My curiosity about such powers of attraction prompted me to research ways of harnessing these magnetic forces and I discovered something radical: that through awareness and the development of our own higher minds our inherent psychic powers can be used to attract the right mate and keep the spark alive in relationships.

Have you ever wondered why you settled with your current partner? Or remembered someone from the past who made a huge impact on you? Did either relationship feel fated? Could they be your soul mate? Maybe you were brought together by pure animal magnetism, or did your relationship start with a compelling rapport based on mutual ideas? Perhaps it was a chance meeting that provoked a sense of overwhelming recognition? Or do you still look back with longing on the one who got away?

Whatever the initial connection, when that 'chemistry' seemingly disappears, or a relationship ends disastrously, we wonder why and question what it was all about. Poems and songs have been written in every era about this soul-wrenching experience of life. Why does love die, or a grand passion end up in rejection, misery, or, even worse, boredom? How can you nurture that bond or re-ignite that spark that first brought you together and fall in love and lust with your loved one all over again?

Imagine for a moment that you have been given a special opportunity to access mystical secrets that can transform your relationships. But first you need to be transported to a new dimension where anything is possible. This place isn't a distant galaxy millions of light years away, but somewhere much closer to home. This privileged and sacred space is within you – an unexplored ancient part of yourself, known as the higher mind. By connecting with its untapped energies you will be able to rediscover a profound relationship with your greatest teacher: yourself. Because the key to understanding and succeeding in relationships lies within our intuitive selves.

Before you exclude yourself from the above, let me confidently say that we all have an innate sixth sense. You may already sense this wise, intuitive voice occasionally trying to exert influence through your hunches, dreams and feelings. But often the stress and fast pace of our modern existence, combined with our own limited thoughts, stop us from being aware of our inner guidance and our abilities remain dimmed. However, there is an easy solution. In the same way that we need to exercise daily to keep our muscles toned and our bodies in good physical health, we also need to use our psychic powers regularly if we want them to work efficiently and guide us through the pitfalls of life. You may think of psychic abilities as something you might use for entertainment, but they can have far-reaching benefits in all aspects of your life. Within these pages you can discover the unique tools that will enable you to connect more fully with your own psychic powerhouse and create the love life that the deepest part of you has always yearned for.

A Loving, Constructive Relationship

What is the purpose and importance of such a relationship? Fortunately, the answers are simple. Two words spring immediately to mind: happiness and healing. A healthy partnership offers you not only the opportunity to share and enjoy intimacy but also to grow and develop as a person.

Relationships are the perfect mirrors for who we are, as through them you reveal your strengths and weaknesses. We know when they work well because we feel contented. A flourishing partnership can provide wonderful support and make life an enjoyable experience. But we also know that love requires a leap of faith and as a consequence relationships are a huge risk too, because, as we're all aware, when they don't work they can make you feel bored, vulnerable, irritable, distressed and at times even traumatised. When, however, we sense a powerful connection with another person something truly extraordinary takes place that lifts us out of our humdrum everyday routine and reminds us of who we truly are.

Let me explain by telling you a familiar story. Ted and Alice had met for the first time. He had just come from a business meeting on the tenth floor of an investment bank and was waiting for the lift to descend. As the lift doors opened, there was Alice. Small and dark, she was no head-turning stunner and certainly nothing like the leggy blonde type he usually went for. But their eyes locked and they couldn't stop smiling. There was no logic to this. They both passed hundreds of people every day of their lives, but this encounter was special, you might say unique. There was a spark, a feeling of familiarity so strong that some unfathomable force seemed to propel them into a sphere of timelessness. From that moment, these two individuals instantly bonded. And that was the beginning of a new partnership.

What they experienced is something we all understand. Whether we have lived it for ourselves or deeply wish for it to happen to us, we call it falling in love. But it is so much more than an overused expression. What happened between these two strangers is a powerful, invisible psychic force, with an energy so strong it is intrinsically palpable to the other. It is a knowing beyond reason, where they are recognising the unique pure soul essence of the other person. And this energy is allied to unconditional love. What this couple sense deep down is a stirring in their spirit that knows that this magnetic attraction has the power to transform them. Not only do they feel a connection with each other, but magically they feel more connected with themselves. This force has acted like an electric shock and woken them up to their intuitive being. As a consequence, the empty void inside has disappeared and, as their happiness spills over, the world becomes a wonderful place.

Whatever the basis of their union, it sounds so predestined it should have a happy ending, shouldn't it? But, sadly, for every Ted and Alice who find lasting happiness there are just as many encounters that end in ruin. Why is it that someone with whom you have pledged undying love, or feel such a compelling attraction to, ends up your worst enemy, squabbling over finances or who last did the washing up? Why does that chemistry have to fizzle out when the habitual patterns of everyday life set in?

It's all down to being in touch with our intuition. Put simply, there is only one fundamental way to attract and develop successful relationships: by strengthening your psychic abilities. You may find this controversial, but before you dismiss it as complete nonsense, think about it. By connecting with your intuition you're connecting with the real you. It is the voice of your soul or higher self. You might think of it as a 'hunch' or a 'feeling' that pays off. But it is our natural state and when we are prompted to listen and express ourselves from this inner sense, we are also more loving, wise, generous and understanding.

Conflicts arise when we ignore our inner voice. When we communicate with fear, anger and selfishness it means our ego has taken over. In this limited state of mind we lose sight of the feelings of others and want everything on our own terms. It is this self-centred perspective that makes us feel like blinkered victims of fate unable to exercise proper judgement. This is the price you pay for losing touch with your higher self, and by doing so you lose your way. It is understandable, then, that with this negative mindset relationships flounder. No wonder so many people think, Why isn't this the person I fell in love with? What we forget is that this defensive behaviour is not the truth, but a manifestation of blind egoism which breeds fear, insecurity and anger. The real beauty still exists inside, but it's easy to forget that when you are confronted with a hostile or indifferent persona who has simply forgotten who they are.

That's why it is so important to focus intuitively on the spark that brought you together and allow it to blossom to its fullest potential. In truth, your partner is your perfect relationship mirror that offers you glimpses of your true self and ultimately has the potential to keep reconnecting you to your spirit within.

Why falling in love triggers intuition

There is a reason why 'falling in love' or 'chemistry' triggers an intuitive connection. Once you know why, you can learn how to keep the psychic flame of passion burning brightly.

This psychic force is awoken because the two energies – love and intuition – come from the same source: the higher mind. One reason why love has this powerful effect is what happens to our consciousness when we feel the impact of strong emotion. First, we need to understand that our minds are pure energy. When we think negatively, our mind energy funnels inwards, creating a pressure on our brain. This causes depression and blocks your psychic powers from flowing. However, when we think happy, loving thoughts our mind energy expands outwards into the universe. This is what happens when there is a strong attraction and we resonate with someone. It is a potent encounter, as when our thoughts and beliefs connect on similar frequencies of recognition we are flooded with positive vibrations and our mind energy immediately opens up.

Scientific research has shown that when the energy of unconditional love is triggered it registers the same brain wave frequency as that of a healer or psychic, which is the vibration that takes you into a powerful healing state, also known as the 'alpha state'. (Refer to the box below for the research on these illuminating studies.) This essentially means that while unconditional love awakens our intuition, linking up to our psychic powers also enables us to feel more compassionate and loving. It therefore has a profound two-way effect.

This explains why telepathic communication is often common between new lovers. The surge of loving feelings acts like an electrical charge and triggers the connection with our intuitive self. Within minutes our consciousness can be transformed from mundane disinterest to a heightened sense of reality where we are seeing life with 'new eyes'.

I'm not talking here about a fleeting dalliance where you fancy someone for a few weeks or a casual one-night stand. Or just responding to someone because they find you attractive and you are eager for some attention or flattery. I'm talking about a real connection with someone. The more compelling the attraction, whether sexual, spiritual or mental, the more we are swamped with positive emotions. It is the 'connection' we are making that brings us together and these feelings – facets of love – are initially unconditional. We haven't had the opportunity to impose our ideas and limitations on to the situation. Or, in some cases, distort the feeling with a projected idea of how we think it will be. We simply 'feel'. And that is why the impact wakes up our sixth sense.

By becoming aware of your thoughts and exercising your higher mind your intuition grows stronger, and the more you use it the more powerful it becomes. As a natural consequence not only do you become more discerning but you feel happier within yourself simply because you are connecting to the voice of your spirit. When this higher self is leading the way contentment is something you can feel whether you are in a relationship or not and stops you from using others to fill an emptiness inside you. Instead of grasping at love to fulfil an inner need you naturally feel more loving and have something to give.

As a result relationships will become more harmonious, because you are connecting with the same source – your spirit. A person who aims to communicate from their intuitive faculties acts with courage, respect, creativity, wisdom and love. Everything good in our lives has its foundations rooted in that instinctive place. That's when things flow smoothly. The results are self-evident. This way of communicating is our natural state and if we nurture it we can continue to connect and empathise with each other more deeply.

The Science of Unconditional Love and Psychic Powers

When we develop our psychic powers our brain wave patterns are also affected, which in turn influence our aura (the energy field that surrounds us). Dr Robert Beck, a nuclear physicist and pioneer in the field of electromedicine, collected important scientific data by measuring the brain waves of healers, ESP readers and psychics. He discovered that our brain waves register a 7.8–8 Hz alpha rhythm when we use our healing or psychic powers. This rhythm synchronises exactly with the fluctuations of the earth's magnetic field, known as the Schumann waves. Linking in with the earth's magnetic field pulses is powerful and healing and gives us a serene, balanced state of mind. Balance is important. As the right side of our brain is receptive, creative and intuitive, and the left side is pragmatic and logical, we need to keep them balanced in order to use our psychic abilities effectively.

Innovative research also proves that when we feel unconditional love in our hearts, this energy resonates with the 7.8–8Hz alpha rhythm of the Schumann waves too. We need to refer to our hearts when we make our most important decisions. We decide what 'feels' right, which is what linking with our intuition also enables us to do.

In 1993 research was conducted at the Institute of HeartMath in Boulder Creek, California which demonstrated that the emotion we call love is the most healing tool to ensure health in body and mind. The research showed that there was a correlation between a subject's mental and emotional states and the frequency spectra of an ECG (electrocardiogram). This means that when the subject felt sincere love, care or appreciation, the spectra changed to a more ordered and coherent frequency distribution. On the other hand, when the subject was frustrated, worried or angry, the ECG spectra were disordered and chaotic. Psychological evaluations confirmed that subjects who felt positive emotions and who produced more coherent ECG frequencies were able to react more calmly to stressful events in everyday life. When we feel unconditional love, with all its facets of generosity, caring, sympathy, empathy and understanding, we send out specific wave forms which, as mentioned earlier, expand our mind consciousness and activate the higher functions in the brain. Like all our thoughts, this emotion is energy, which travels out into time and space and affects other people. The more positive our thoughts, the more harmonious our relationships become.

Your prescription for supernatural love

So what does all this mean? Within these chapters is the opportunity to discover the psychic tools to transform any obstacles in your close encounters. Just think how incredible your relationships could be if you could forge a magical alliance with your partner. The potential is huge. You could quickly resolve conflicts by meeting up in your dreams, or develop telepathy and become more in sync to build a closer intimacy. You could understand the power of your thoughts and influence your partner's mood by focusing your mind. Learn about the deeper forces of psychic sex, and what happens to our psychic energy when we make love. Discover how to access latent psychic forces that have the power to reawaken passion and strengthen your connection. Or if you feel you drifted together and there is no real connection between you, if you want to remain together discover how to create and nurture a powerful bond.

Does it sound too good to be true? Well, this is no futuristic fantasy. Let's face it, we all have one thing in common: the desire for the perfect partner, with the right chemistry who loves us unconditionally and understands us like no one else.

That doesn't mean you have to be with Mr or Ms Perfect who agrees robotically with everything you say. If that were so, how would you evolve and understand other points of views? The relationships I want for you are not about skating over the surface and being content with a pleasant, convenient life. This is for the pioneers among you who want your partnerships to be based on a higher ground: real soul-to-soul communication, heartfelt passion and genuine honesty.

Whatever your circumstances, if you are willing, you are about to embark on an exciting adventure that will change the way you think for ever. By looking at some of the more potent ways in which we connect, you can discover the dynamics of whether you have a powerful soul mate link, a past life connection, potent sexual magnetism or mental synergy. Maybe you'll find the courage to move forward if you know you're in an unhealthy liaison that's reached stalemate. Using practical exercises throughout the book you can hone and heighten your intuition and harness the powerful energy that lies within. These specific techniques will enhance your psychic awareness and by applying them to your relationships, you will be able to attract, develop or transform a bond that will bring a deeper connection of trust, empathy, honesty and unconditional love. I promise you that it can happen. You have the knowledge within you – you just need to know how to use it.

Keep a sense of adventure

Relax and enjoy the exercises throughout this book. In fact you should always keep a sense of fun and adventure. When you are working with your own psychic powers, you should do the opposite to what you think. Trying too hard to achieve results is a turnoff to your higher mind and your partner; tapping in to your intuition will teach you a lot about developing a loving relationship. With any kind of partnership you have to focus on your goal and put in the effort, and it is the same with your relationship with your higher mind. Just like communicating with a lover, if you get too needy and push too hard to make things work, you fall into the realm of the lower mind, which means controlling and possessing the object of your desire through insecurity and fear. Then the relationship gets stuck and stops flourishing. For the best results our relationship with our instinctive self needs to be approached in the same way as we would a loving partnership – with the spirit of adventure, optimism, trust and an open mind.

Keep a diary of your journey

Note every experience that happens as you read this book and value this document as a testimony to the higher development of your relationship. It will also enable you to refer back as you work through the book to see how you're progressing. By keeping an account of your new thoughts and beliefs, dreams, insights, hunches and coincidences through good times and bad as you do the exercises to heal your partnership, you will continually discover aspects about who you are and how your partnership is evolving. You can look back on accounts of what your relationship means to you and what you consider to be your goals and aspirations. Intuitive awareness and a deep psychic bond don't happen all at once; it is a process that unfolds, sometimes rapidly but sometimes more gradually over a period of time. Everything you understand will go towards a bigger picture to create the supernatural relationship you deserve.

Your Psychic Journey

The first step will be a journey to discover more about who you are: your thoughts and feelings and what they say about you. Once you are aware of the way you think, you can begin to understand why you have attracted certain people into your life and what you want to achieve in a partnership. You can then move on to a questionnaire that is specifically tailored to enable you to understand the way in which you and your partner connect. Once you have your answers you are ready to launch yourself into the orbit of your higher mind with your compass to direct you to those chapters uniquely designed to strengthen and rekindle the spark of energy within your particular relationship. Only then can you begin to learn the psychic tools to invest in your relationship – and discover how you can be the very best supernatural lover.

A commitment to yourself

I have a dream, my very own personal vision and it's one that's shared within our collective unconscious: that each and every one of you realises your greatest potential by becoming the person you always wanted to be, one who is in touch with their creative, intuitive self – the voice of your spirit – and therefore fulfilled and awakened to what life and love mean. Imagine a world where you can feel happy just for the sake of it. You have a zest for life because you really appreciate what your life is for. A person like this gives love unconditionally because, by listening to their intuitive selves, they are in touch with who they are. A person like this is fulfilled even when they spend time alone because they feel contented with who they are. This person is you. The wiser, boundless you that you have temporarily forgotten. But by picking up this book you have decided to remind yourself how to find the way back. Through developing your intuitive self you develop your capacity to love unconditionally not just another person, but the adventure of life itself.

So take off your mask and start living life with your intuitive self in the driving seat. You are not trying to be someone else but becoming who you already are. And with that goal in mind you are already a supernatural lover.

But at this point I need your commitment. Not to me or anyone else, but to yourself. This is your chance to stop being a victim of fate. You have the opportunity to get off that merry-go-round of isolation, misunderstandings and conflict that lead to ill-fated affairs of the heart. If you want to transform your love life to one that is deeply fulfilling on all levels, then you must make a promise to yourself. If you pledge to keep an open mind and an adventurous spirit and let your higher intuitive self lead the way, you will experience an enlightening way of relating to others. One that will enable you not only to feel more connected to your loved ones, but also, more importantly, more connected to yourself.

Prepare for an adventure. Your time is now and you will soon discover just how much power you have to orchestrate your own destiny and transform your relationships into deep and loving bonds. But before you go any further, you need to delve into the recesses of your mind and implement some profound changes from deep within your subconscious.

ATTRACTION IS ALL IN THE MIND

2

UNDERSTANDING THE POWER OF YOUR THOUGHTS

Tell me who admires you and who loves you and I will tell you who you are.
CHARLES AUGUSTIN SAINTE-BEUVE, 1804–69, FRENCH ACADEMIC AND WRITER

In this chapter we are going to look at the first and most important building block of a loving partnership: the relationship we have with ourselves. This relationship should be your most loving and compassionate, simply because, by being a best friend and carer to yourself, you create a constructive blueprint for every relationship you have. So what is your blueprint? It is your legacy to yourself programmed from all your experiences of life, a conglomeration of all your thoughts and feelings, conscious and unconscious, which includes your ingrained beliefs, desires and fears, and it's contained in the mind energy surrounding you, known as an aura. Every experience you've ever had will be held within your auric energy field. The health of your aura, just like the condition of your body, is essential to your happiness, because every thought and emotion we have radiates vibrations that attract like-minded people and repel others. The basis, then of using your psychic powers to transform relationships must first begin with a journey into your own powerful mind.

Your Auric Blueprint

When we tune in psychically to someone we are sensing information contained in the human magnetic field – the aura. This mind energy field can be seen by sensitives as a light or grey colour, but there are specific devices that allow anyone to see the aura, such as Kirlian photography which reveals myriad shades of the colour spectrum, depending on the mood or emotion we are feeling.

There are seven different levels to our aura, which contain information on every aspect of who we are as people. This ranges from our physical health, sexuality, subconscious fears, happy memories, or even our inspirations – in fact every belief and emotion you experience will be revealed.

How we connect: The Chakra Energy Points

You also need to know how we connect through our energy power points in our relationships. The seven levels to our aura also connect to our physical body at seven energy points located along the spine (See diagram page 18). These points are our power centres, known as chakras. Just like the aura they are invisible unless seen by the sensitive eye of a psychic and look a little like whirling lotus petals.

They start with a base chakra, located at the bottom of your spine and end with a crown chakra in the dome of your head. Just like the levels of the aura they relate to the physical (first auric level) right through to the higher spiritual mind (seventh auric level).

1. ***Base chakra,*** *located at the bottom of the spine, relates to our physical body. The colour associated with this chakra is red.*
2. ***Splenic chakra,*** *located in the small of the back. It relates to our vitality and sexuality. The associated colour is orange.*
3. ***Solar plexus chakra,*** *associated with the stomach and is located in the centre of the spinal area. It relates to our emotions and lower mind to do with intellect and rational thought. The colour is yellow.*
4. ***Heart chakra,*** *located between our shoulder blades in line with our heart. It is to do with our feelings of unconditional love and affection. The colour is green.*
5. ***Throat chakra,*** *located at the base of our skull in the throat area. It is to do with all areas of communication and speaking from our true selves. The colour is blue.*
6. ***Third eye chakra,*** *located in the centre of the brow and relates to clairvoyance, intuition and healing. The colour is indigo.*
7. ***Crown chakra,*** *located in the dome of the head. It relates to spiritual experiences and enlightenment. The colour is violet.*

The Power of our Thoughts

As our thoughts and feelings change, so the information in our aura will reflect our current thinking. The auric field reaches three and a half feet in most individuals, but can treble in size when someone is particularly creative, psychic or spiritually aware. We carry this information with us all the time and this explains why, even if you don't believe you are psychic, we can often take an instant dislike to or feel a strong affinity with certain people. This happens because each couple in a relationship connects through energy frequencies on one or more levels

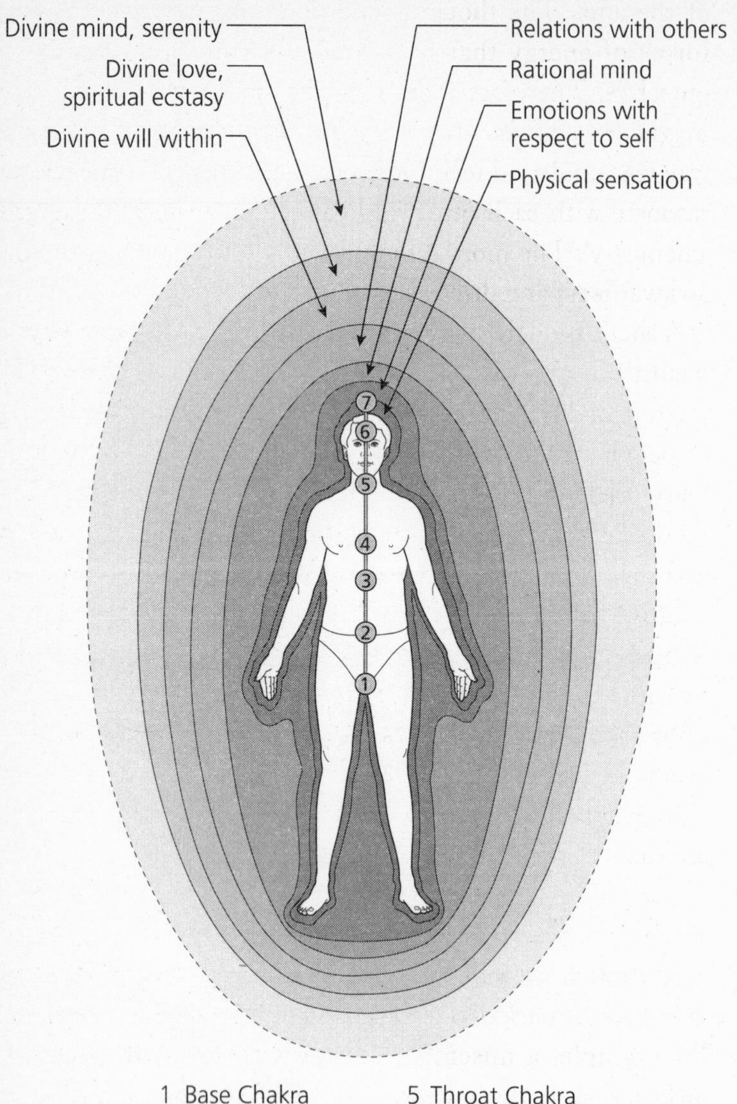

1 Base Chakra
2 Splenic chakra
3 Solar plexus chakra
4 Heart chakra
5 Throat Chakra
6 Third eye chakra
7 Crown chakra

Your Auric Energy Fields and Chakra Points

of the aura. The thoughts and emotions we have are simply forms of energy that have an impact on other people and ourselves. Therefore every thought, emotion and word has a magnetic pull. The more similar you are to someone else in the way you think and feel, the more those energy frequencies will resonate with each other and create that magical thing called 'chemistry'. The more different you are to someone, the more awkwardness and disparity will be felt.

A single thought is very powerful and may affect not only your health but also influence the way you behave. We are all a mixture of different emotions, but think about the various types of people you know who you might classify as 'easy-going' or 'fiery', 'defensive' or 'dynamic', a 'survivor' or a 'victim'. These modes of behaviour will stem from their consistent thoughts, and therefore reveal how they react to circumstances and how healthy they are. To a psychic, the aura of a depressive or 'stressed' individual may reveal dark areas of negative thought or show colours that reveal signs of imbalance. Positive and optimistic thoughts lead to balanced, productive reactions to events in life, and good health. This is reflected in a strong, vibrant aura that can often fill a room with energy so that others see them as dynamic or charismatic.

Appearances can be deceptive, but we all 'pick up' on someone's state of mind by the feelings that emanate from them even though we may initially try and push that instinctive reaction to the back of our minds. This natural 'sensor' will make, for example, a miserable person with low self-esteem feel awkward around someone who is positive and happy, but will produce an affinity in others who are like-minded.

Mind Energy Connection

All this is telling us that what we are attracted to in someone in fact reveals a lot about ourselves and the similarities in the way we think or feel. If we gel with someone, our mind energy is reaching out and connecting with that person on one or more levels of our aura. The more common ground we share the more chemistry we feel. This is because our energy is attracted to aspects similar to itself, such as having similar goals in life, a similar childhood or the same attitude to sex, which can provoke a spark or a strong feeling of resonance.

For example, someone with a strong intellect who loves to study may converse easily on the mental level with a partner who has the same leanings and they will have a fantastic rapport. But if other levels of this couple's auras are at odds with each other – for instance one of them is physically fit and optimistic and the other isn't – it may mean that sexually and emotionally they are not well suited and they would have problems in this area despite their intellectual rapport. But these levels can be easily rebalanced, and a synergy created, if they work on strengthening the weaker aspects of themselves to mirror their partner's feelings. Even in the case of 'opposites attract' you can guarantee that on some level, whether sexual, spiritual or creative, a couple will have a strong mutual understanding that has drawn them together.

Our everyday expressions such as 'we gelled', 'connected', 'attracted like magnets', 'were on the same wavelength', 'on the same level', 'were in sync' or 'clicked' reveal exactly what happens with our energy when we connect with a similar mindset: it is our intuitive feeling of being pulled towards a similar force. Recall someone with whom you really gelled, focus on the attraction and note the 'connections' you made on various levels that gave you that special magnetic feeling.

When Jenny, a television researcher, met Steve, a producer, they clicked instantly. They couldn't stop talking and afterwards Jenny felt as if she were walking on air. They seemed to share the same creative ideas (seventh level of the aura) and they were disciplined and did their jobs well (fifth level of the aura). Both had read and understood the same types of philosophical books (sixth level) and they enjoyed study and research in their jobs (third level). This provoked a heightened sense of 'belonging together' when they communicated because their energy was flowing between them on so many levels.

This sort of energy flow also explains why, despite feeling a powerful chemistry with someone, they are not necessarily the ideal person for us. Parts of your mind energy (thoughts) are simply recognising another's thought energy, hence the expression 'Like attracts like' or 'Birds of a feather flock together'. This is not so constructive when you are both responding unconsciously to old childhood issues, destructive emotions from a past life or a negative self-esteem – unless we take on the challenge and learn to become aware of these patterns and heal them. It is those of similar mind energy to ourselves who can often press our buttons the most, mirroring back to us our strengths but also our weaknesses. This means that we can love someone beyond reason, because we feel such a strong synergy, but they may still at times prove challenging and difficult. That is why powerful attractions are our most magnifying mirrors. In the same way we can't see or improve what we look like without looking at our own reflection, we can't see our character faults and damaging thought patterns until we see them reflected back at us in our partnerships. Remember, it is for our own improvement and growth that we need to keep seeing who we are – reflected back in our magnetic attractions.

Your Connections

Now you can see why you have a synergy with certain individuals. Take note, though, that the energy connections I am talking about are not simply a response to someone who found you appealing. It is the people for whom *you* feel a strong affinity or compelling attraction who will tell you the truth about yourself.

Many people are unaware of the way they think, and react automatically to people and events in their lives, forgetting that they have 50 per cent of the responsibility for the outcome of a situation. I am inviting you to take control of your destiny.

Instead of blaming a partner for their weaknesses, look at your own attitudes, characteristics and beliefs and begin to heal them. Bear in mind that you are strongly attracted to someone because they are a reflection of the different aspects of you. If you don't like what you see, look at the selfishness, aggression or laziness in their behaviour and change your attitudes and beliefs. Your new beliefs and thoughts will either create harmony or you will attract someone else who will reflect your current state. This process continues until we transform the negative thoughts and beliefs within ourselves.

By being consciously aware of how you think, you take responsibility for the way your personal relationships are affected. By disciplining your thoughts, you take control of your mind instead of allowing it to enslave you. The very cornerstone of this book, then, is that your thoughts are the foundation of any relationship. The more conscious you become of the way you think, the more constructive your relationships will be. And the more your aura will reflect this new information.

Transforming your mind energy to attract healthy loving partnerships

Everyone has the potential to strengthen the different levels of their aura by being aware of how their current thoughts and emotions will be reflected in their everyday life. Every action you decide to take, from ending a relationship to going to the gym, stems from a thought, and any thought can be changed to a more constructive one. An entire book could be written on understanding our energy field but I have devised a questionnaire that will help you focus on the different levels of your mind and how they are working for you at the moment. It will enable you to take a good look at yourself holistically, so that all aspects of who you are – physically, emotionally and spiritually – are taken into account and nourished. By looking at the strengths and weaknesses in your mind energy you can explore the way you think and redress the balance. You can stop being a victim of old beliefs and have the kind of relationships you want. Crucially, strengthening the higher levels of your mind (the fifth, sixth and seventh levels of your aura) will develop your psychic powers and allow you to listen to your inner voice. The more balanced you are on your physical, emotional and spiritual levels, the more balanced will be the partner you attract. Equally, the more productive a current relationship will be. It stands to reason that if you want someone who is generous, kind and intellectual with a healthy self-esteem and spirituality, then you need to generate those qualities in yourself first.

Rebalance your aura: A questionnaire to reveal your thoughts, feelings and beliefs

The following questionnaire will enable you to explore the attitudes, thoughts and feelings that are reflected in the seven levels of your aura.

This is an in-depth exercise that will help you gain a valuable understanding of yourself and much needed clarity before going any further. Gaining insights into the way you think is crucial if you want to develop your personal relationships successfully.

The questionnaire may look extensive, but there are only thirty-five questions in all, five under each level. Simply note whether a), b) or c) is the most applicable to you. Under each set of questions you will find the scores. Add up the values corresponding to your chosen answers, and find out which level of your aura needs strengthening. You need only set aside around fifteen minutes to answer all the questions and work out your scores.

As you work through each section, your answers will reveal your strengths and weaknesses on every level of your energy field; then you can take note of the beneficial suggestions at your own pace. You may find it useful to redo the quiz or refer back to the conclusions as you go through the book.

Remember, this is not an exam. Be honest with yourself and don't feel competitive or stressed. You are not being judged. Each level is just another facet of your mind and when you have finished you will be more aware of the way you think and clearer about replacing old, limited attitudes and thoughts that hold you back with more expansive, productive ones.

FIRST LEVEL: Physical sensation

This relates to your basic needs on a physical level including all pleasurable and painful sensations.

1. ***How much exercise do you do daily?***

☐ a) *I walk for one hour or more a day.*

☐ b) *I go to the gym several times a week; or I play sport; or I take dance classes; or I do yoga.*

☐ c) *I walk only to take the tube/bus/car to go to work and then slump on the settee when I get home; or take no exercise at all.*

2. ***What kind of diet do you have?***

☐ a) *I have times when I eat healthily but generally eat on the run, with cups of coffee and fast food snacks to keep me going.*

☐ b) *I generally aim to eat plenty of fresh fruit and vegetables every day with minimal processed foods.*

☐ c) *I am not interested in food, or I am a frequent dieter.*

3. ***How healthy are you?***

☐ a) *I feel weak and fragile. I often get ill and have to take time off work.*

☐ b) *I rarely get ill, I have a lot of energy and a healthy constitution.*

☐ c) *I never have to take time off work but I get frequent colds; or I don't get ill because stress keeps me going.*

4. ***How sensual are you?***

☐ a) *I am tactile, enjoy giving/receiving massage and making love if in a relationship.*

☐ b) *I don't enjoy being touched or touching others.*

☐ c) *I have been celibate for more than one year but still enjoy massage and affection.*

5. *What are your sleeping patterns?*

☐ a) *I always sleep well and feel rested in the morning.*

☐ b) *I sometimes have restless nights and feel exhausted in the mornings; or I sleep too much.*

☐ c) *I suffer with insomnia; or I need sleep all the time.*

Scoring

1.	*a) 5*	*b) 20*	*c) 0*
2.	*a) 5*	*b) 10*	*c) 0*
3.	*a) 0*	*b) 10*	*c) 5*
4.	*a) 10*	*b) 10*	*c) 5*
5.	*a) 10*	*b) 5*	*c) 0*

Your first level explained

0–35: Weak first level

You have a weak first level, which means you are not connected properly with your body. A lack of physical exercise is probably the main cause. As a result you will often feel physically weak and may suffer with lethargy or ill health. You may not enjoy sexual intimacy, exercise or even eating, and may consider them as experiences to be endured. Our connection to our physical needs will vary from person to person. For example, you may love exercising but be disinterested in sex – in which case pay more attention to your sensuality and perhaps start with a massage or aromatherapy treatment to relax and get in touch with your needs on this level. Or you may enjoy food but not feel inclined to exercise, so focus on doing yoga, aerobics or find time to walk regularly. Those with eating disorders will have a weak first level as will someone in a sedentary job, such as a hairdresser or an office worker. If you are in a job like this it is essential that you play some sport, walk or get some other exercise rather than going straight home to veg out on the settee. Otherwise your first level will become even weaker and you will become more prone to ill health or insomnia as stress builds up and is unable to be released. You may also feel over-sensitive or unstable as you don't have a strong mind–body connection and it will be harder for you to use your intuition and creative forces usefully.

40–60: Strong first level

Your first level is very strong and this means you feel physically strong and have a healthy constitution with a lot of vitality. Athletes, dancers and those whose jobs involve physical labour usually have a well-developed first level thanks to the regular exercise. Your thoughts on the physical aspects of your life are obviously positive. You radiate a grounded inner strength, so keep up the good work and continue to take care of yourself. Connecting with your body will also give you a strong mind–body link, eliminating tension and stress from your body, so that intuition can flow more easily.

To ensure a healthy first level

The first level of your aura can become weak whenever you are not taking enough care of your body's physical needs. This could happen to anyone at any time. Pay attention to this level when any traumatic incident happens, when a relationship breaks up or you are experiencing conflicts with anyone. It is during these stressful periods that we can forget to eat healthily, and our habits, exercise and sleeping patterns are disrupted. Recovering from illness or changing your job from an active one to a more sedentary role are also periods in your life when your first level may suffer. However strong you've discovered your first level to be, keep a regular check of your thoughts towards your physical needs and write them down in your diary. If you find yourself thinking negative thoughts consciously replace them with more constructive ones.

What is your attitude to exercise, sex and food? If you have an unhealthy diet, look at the thoughts that provoke you to eat in that way. If you think you haven't enough time to eat properly and have to eat on the run, make something the night before. Healthy food can be quick and easy to prepare, like a tuna sandwich or grilled fish. It is our excuses and attitudes – mere thoughts – that lead us down a certain pathway. Perhaps you prefer not to exercise because you are too busy, or have a bad back or any other number of excuses. Ask yourself why and think positively for the sake of your health. If you haven't got time to go to the gym, then walk to the shops instead of driving. Your body needs to be kept active, not only to keep you toned and energised but to eliminate tension that we accumulate every day.

Remember

- Exercise regularly
- Enjoy a healthy diet
- Take time for focused intimacy with a partner.
- Make time for massage, bathing and other sensual pleasures.
- Ensure you get the right amount of restful sleep for you.

SECOND LEVEL: Self-Worth

This level is about the emotions we have towards ourselves and whether you accept and love yourself in a healthy way.

1. ***How attractive do you feel?***

☐ *a) My feelings of ugliness affect my life and stop me doing what I want; or I hate looking at myself in the mirror.*

☐ *b) I feel too fat/thin/not perfect by society's standards and sometimes this means my appearance plays on my mind.*

☐ *c) I feel very attractive.*

2. ***How happy are you?***

☐ *a) I am happy and positive most of the time regardless of what's happening.*

☐ *b) I suffer with very bad depression and it affects my life.*

☐ *c) I sometimes feel down, but I can snap out of it.*

3. ***How lovable do you believe yourself to be?***

☐ *a) I believe I am completely worthy of being loved.*

☐ *b) I have ups and downs, but generally I feel good about who I am.*

☐ *c) If someone is loving towards me, I feel they must have something wrong with them.*

4. ***How self-critical are you?***

☐ *a) I often feel self-hatred and criticise my looks and how my life is; or I believe I am a bad person; or I am not aware of how I feel about myself.*

☐ *b) I enjoy feeling good so I try to avoid any uncomfortable feelings. I might drink, take drugs, smoke or overeat to feel better.*

☐ *c) I feel good about myself most of the time and give myself positive feedback about my looks and how my life is.*

5. ***How well do you take care of yourself?***

☐ *a) I never have a chance to take care of myself, I'm always busy; or I consider it to be self-indulgent; or other things are more important.*

☐ b) *I regularly take time out for myself by focusing on me, whether it be the hairdresser, having manicures, facials, or even an hour in the bath with a good book.*

☐ c) *I occasionally grab some time to do something for myself.*

Scoring

1.	*a)* 0	*b)* 5	*c)* 10
2.	*a)* 10	*b)* 0	*c)* 5
3.	*a)* 10	*b)* 5	*c)* 0
4.	*a)* 0	*b)* 5	*c)* 10
5.	*a)* 0	*b)* 10	*c)* 5

Your second level explained

0–25: Weak second level

Many people tend to have weakness in the second level of their aura as this level is about loving and accepting yourself as you are – something many people in today's critical society find difficult to achieve. Blockages and weaknesses in the second level arise when we suppress negative feelings about ourselves and don't acknowledge or express them. This can make you melancholy and can lead to self-hatred, depression or, in some cases, suicidal feelings.

A weakness also occurs when you are unaware of how you feel because you are avoiding your emotions or going into denial, pretending the bad feeling doesn't exist by hiding behind a façade, for example, by being outwardly cheerful but deep down feeling resentful and miserable. We need to be aware of the emotion in order to experience it and let it go, otherwise it will become blocked. The effects of denial are commonplace, as many people use drugs, alcohol, overeating, sex or overwork as a way of escaping the pain of their emotions. An ebb and flow of negative and positive feelings about ourselves is natural as we clear out the emotional effects of everyday life.

30–50: Strong second level

You are a rare breed! You have a strong second level, which means a healthy sense of self-worth. You feel comfortable in your own company, even when you are completely alone. You are able to express your emotions and tend to want open communication with someone rather than pretend everything is okay. You are genuinely happy most of the time and have an optimistic attitude to life. This is enormously helpful for your psychic development, as your mind energy is expansive and keeps your intuitive energy flowing.

To ensure a healthy second level

Your second level can weaken whenever you are not taking enough care of your emotional needs towards yourself. We need to keep a check on this aspect of our minds, as we are more sensitive than we realise and are often affected by stress and other people. Arguments with work colleagues, conflicts in relationships or even feeling ignored can all take their toll on our self-esteem. Whatever circumstances arise in your life, try not to get into the habit of criticising yourself and creating negativity. Whatever other people say to you, don't take it personally or feel attacked. Be aware that their thoughts say more about themselves and their own negative patterns. Try to have honest and assertive (but not aggressive or confrontational) communication when you feel upset so that you release the negative emotion.

Note when your thoughts are self-critical. Perhaps you are being overly judgemental by thinking, I'm not good enough, I can't do anything right, or I'm fat, ugly or useless. Be vigilant and write down these thoughts and then change them to, 'I am good enough, I do the best I can. I am a beautiful, kind and loving person with many talents.' Focus on creative pursuits such as writing, painting or pottery to express how you feel and release the negative emotion. And don't turn to addictive props like overeating, alcohol or drugs to escape your sorrows. Deal with your feelings today.

Remember

- Acknowledge how you feel.
- Express your feelings through creativity.
- Don't mask your feelings with addictions.
- Strive for honest communication with yourself and others.
- Think positive thoughts about yourself.
- Make quality time to pamper yourself.

THIRD LEVEL: Rational mind

This relates to your needs on the rational level of your mind and reflects how much you study and use your intellect.

1. ***Do you enjoy intellectual pursuits?***

☐ *a) I love learning and always enjoy studying and researching different things of interest.*

☐ *b) I don't consider myself to be particularly intellectual and I'm not interested in studying or learning about new things.*

☐ *c) I don't actively study but my job/hobby involves researching subjects or studying.*

2. ***What are your thinking processes?***

☐ *a) I tend to spend too much time over-analysing or brooding on things.*

☐ b) *I occasionally worry about things.*
☐ c) *I think positively and go with the flow.*

3. ***How decisive are you?***
☐ a) *I'm very decisive and act quickly when I need to.*
☐ b) *I occasionally find it hard to make decisions.*
☐ c) *I am very indecisive and often lose opportunities because I can't make up my mind.*

4. ***How positive are you about people and situations?***
☐ a) *If I'm honest I'm often quite bitchy and tend to malign people behind their backs.*
☐ b) *If someone is negative or I don't feel comfortable, I avoid them rather than be malicious about them.*
☐ c) *I try to think the best of people and say constructive, positive things.*

5. ***Do you have a good measure of logic and intuition?***
☐ a) *I feel I am pretty intuitive but I tend never to act on it.*
☐ b) *I prefer a logical approach.*
☐ c) *I tend to go with my hunches and instinct, which pays off in practical ways.*

Scoring

1.	*a) 10*	*b) 0*	*c) 5*
2.	*a) 0*	*b) 5*	*c) 10*
3.	*a) 10*	*b) 5*	*c) 0*
4.	*a) 0*	*b) 5*	*c) 10*
5.	*a) 5*	*b) 0*	*c) 10*

Your third level explained

0–25: Weak third level

When this level shows weakness it means that you are not using your mental faculties to their best potential. You need mental stimulation. You don't have to do a degree or become the new Einstein, but simply develop your capacity to learn. Without exercising this part of your mind you may suffer from stagnant mental energy. The knock-on effects are that you will lack clarity or mental agility and will find it hard to learn new subjects. It may be difficult for you to pull your thoughts together at times, as you feel confused, muddled or in a mental fog. You may find that your memory gets worse, as you are not using this level of your mind effectively. This will also mean that your intuition is not in balance with your logic, and you may find it difficult to think on your feet or have the clarity to act on a hunch. You may be over-analytical, brooding too much about negative thoughts.

30–50: Strong third level

You have a strong third level, which means you have a healthy mind that serves you well. You enjoy studying different things and have an interest in learning, so you have mental clarity and balance. You also tend to think positively which helps expand your mind energy. Because you regularly stimulate this part of your mind, you have a good memory, can act quickly on a hunch and are known for your quicksilver thought processes. All these aspects, coupled with the fact that you tend to think in a positive way, means that you have a balanced mind that can keep things in perspective. You are mentally strong and more able to cope with stressful situations in a calm way. A strong third level is essential for helping your intuition to flow, as positive thoughts with a good balance of your yin and yang energy ensure that your mind energy continues to expand outwards and release mental tension.

To ensure a healthy third level

This level becomes weak whenever we stop learning about new things, over-analyse or constantly have negative thoughts. Pay particular attention to the times in your life when there are major changes. However intellectual you are, this level can weaken when you become ill or perhaps give up your job to go travelling, or retire; indeed at any time when you don't stretch this part of your mind. Look at your thoughts in this area. If you don't choose to study anything new, ask yourself if you learn in other aspects of your life: do you watch documentaries or pick up non-fiction books to understand different philosophies or cultures? If you aren't taking an interest, look at your thoughts as to why you don't want to and write them down. Do you see yourself as more physical than intellectual? Have you blocked yourself from learning because you don't see yourself as clever enough? Replace those thoughts with ones that have a healthy interest in acquiring knowledge. If it feels difficult, choose a subject that you have always had an interest in – there must be one, whether it's French, nineteenth-century history, mechanics or cooking – and take an evening class in it.

Stagnation in this level can also occur when we think in an overly negative way. Stress can make us feel unbalanced and there are times when we may obsess or over-analyse things. Negativity also includes maligning people behind their backs. Confronting someone in an appropriate way (non-aggressively) to their face releases negative energy and creates honest communication. Make a point of thinking positively and if you are over-focusing on a problem then take some time out and relax, listen to some music or absorb yourself in learning something new. This will help bring back a sense of perspective.

Remember

- Keep learning about new things.
- Keep a sense of perspective.
- Think positively about other people.
- Be optimistic about your life.
- Don't over-analyse things or obsess.

FOURTH LEVEL: Relationships with others

This level relates to the need we have to give unconditional love and affection to others.

1. ***Describe your platonic relationships with others***

☐ a) *I am a people person, I love being around lots of people whether at work or play, and my friends and family make up a big part of my life.*

☐ b) *I can be sociable when I'm in the mood, but I'm also a private person with only a few choice close friends, but enjoy a close family unit.*

☐ c) *I tend to be a loner and find it hard to make friends, and have tentative ties to my family.*

2. ***What's your attitude towards intimate relationships?***

☐ a) *Most sexual relationships are more trouble than they are worth. I always end up in a stressful situation or feel abandoned and unloved.*

☐ b) *I am in a strongly committed loving relationship.*

☐ c) *I tend to have a lot of short-lived relationships that don't last but I strive for something more long term; or I am celibate because I choose to be at the moment.*

3. ***What type of work do you do?***

- ☐ *a) I work in the caring/service profession e.g. nurse/counsellor/with children.*
- ☐ *b) I prefer to work alone when I can get on at my own pace; or I work with other people but would prefer not to.*
- ☐ *c) I work with lots of people in a busy office and like to work as part of a team.*

4. ***How affectionate/loving are you?***

- ☐ *a) I am generous, affectionate, tactile and loving towards lots of people.*
- ☐ *b) I'm a private person. I'm not outwardly demonstrative or tactile at all.*
- ☐ *c) I am affectionate and loving to a close circle of friends/partner/children and family but no one else.*

5. ***Which statement most strongly relates to you?***

- ☐ *a) People say I can seem quite unapproachable and aloof – or spiky.*
- ☐ *b) People say I am open, warm and tactile with most people.*
- ☐ *c) People say I can be a little reserved with people until I get to know them better.*

Scoring

1.	*a)* 20	*b)* 5	*c)* 0
2.	*a)* 0	*b)* 10	*c)* 5
3.	*a)* 10	*b)* 0	*c)* 5
4.	*a)* 10	*b)* 0	*c)* 5
5.	*a)* 0	*b)* 10	*c)* 5

Your fourth level explained

0–30: Weak Fourth Level

Your fourth level is weak which means that relationships aren't as important to you as they might be to others. Often it can be hard for people to admit to weakness in this area as we all like to think of ourselves as loving individuals who give. But this level shows you are not governed by your heart or thoughts of other people's feelings. Perhaps you may be a loner or choose to be celibate, believing that relationships are more trouble than they are worth. Are you intolerant of having to share with someone? You might find it difficult to give generously to others or put them first. Or maybe you find it hard to show a bit of kindness or comfort to someone when they need it. You may prefer to live and work alone or in some cases dislike the idea of socialising with a group of people. This is because other people's fourth level may be stronger than yours and while you may think that other people are tiring, it may simply be that their heart energy is overpowering you, which can make you feel overwhelmed if you are around others for too long.

Look at the kind of person you turn to in a crisis. Why do you look to them for support? What qualities do they have? Do they seem to care and support you? Emulate them and return the favour. Show unconditional love as much as you can in terms of sympathy, understanding, generosity and kindness towards your friends, family and children in order to develop your fourth level. Real love means not expecting anything in return and putting someone else's needs before your own.

35–60: Strong Fourth Level

This level is strong and healthy. This means you are generous, giving, enjoy many friendships and prefer a close family unit. Your friends and family make up a big part of your life. Having a loving, intimate relationship is of prime importance to you and you will want to give this much of your time, ensuring that your partner has a lot of attention. Love is the most important thing in your life. You are a typical 'people person' and enjoy others' company. You are probably known as a good listener, caring and thoughtful. People turn to you for support in a crisis because they know you care. You may work in a caring industry or in the service profession where you are surrounded by people. With a strong fourth level you will often feel connected to your intuitive voice as you are in touch with your emotions, and your mind energy is expansive as it's turned towards helping others rather than focused on yourself.

To ensure a healthy fourth level

We all need to learn to give more love and affection to other people in our lives. The stressful society that we live in means that we can often become selfish and consumed with our own problems. To keep this level strong put other people's needs before your own at times or do something for someone else's happiness just for the pleasure it gives them. This doesn't mean you have to become a doormat. We all need boundaries and to learn when to say 'no' but we also have a huge capacity to give.

Look at your thoughts in this area. Do you like others to be happy? How much do you put yourself out for others, or show affection to someone? Find the thought behind an action. Is it that you can't be bothered or you're to busy focusing on what you want? Or do you think it will go unappreciated? It's too easy to be selfish. Look at how you think and change it. Often giving generously is a great cure for self-pity or emotional turmoil as we focus our energy on someone else. When you give unconditionally, it shouldn't matter if people appreciate it or don't respond graciously. Give for the pleasure of giving, without wanting to receive. Write down 'I want to give, I am generous, I am loving' and act generously when you're in circumstances where you can show affection, so that you programme your thoughts to be more loving. Don't wait for someone to show you appreciation, generosity or friendship. Learn to give first.

Remember

- Aim to show unconditional love to your family and friends.
- Be aware of other people's needs.
- Be generous.
- Be a good listener.
- Put yourself out for others.

FIFTH LEVEL: Divine order within

This is the level about the need to feel connected to the greater pattern of life.

1. ***What's your time-keeping like?***

☐ *a) I am always late and it gets me into trouble.*
☐ *b) I'm reliable and always on time, or I'm always early.*
☐ *c) I try to be on time, but can often arrive late.*

2. ***How tidy are you?***

☐ *a) I hate housekeeping and my home is always in a mess.*
☐ *b) I aim to be clean and tidy. I believe in the art of feng shui and try to keep clutter and untidiness at bay.*
☐ *c) I'm obsessively tidy and clean.*

3. ***How do you feel about rules?***

☐ a) *I don't always agree with them, but I accept them.*

☐ b) *I hate conforming and rebel against so-called society's rules. You should follow your own ideas.*

☐ c) *I believe it is important to have a sense of structure in your life; without order there would be chaos.*

4. ***Do you feel connected to the greater purpose of life?***

☐ a) *When you read this question do you think, stop trying to define me, or This doesn't make any sense to me, or I feel like I am a cog in the wheel of life, going through the motions.*

☐ b) *I don't know what I should be doing, but I want to find out what it is.*

☐ c) *I definitely feel I am on the right path. I know where I'm going and doing what I'm meant to be doing.*

5. ***What's your attitude to work?***

☐ a) *I believe that you should be the best you can be. If a job's worth doing, it's worth doing well.*

☐ b) *I've frequently been fired.*

☐ c) *I just go through the motions when it comes to work.*

Scoring

1.	a) 0	b) 10	c) 5
2.	a) 0	b) 10	c) 5
3.	a) 5	b) 0	c) 10
4.	a) 0	b) 5	c) 10
5.	a) 10	b) 0	c) 5

Your fifth level explained

0–25: Weak fifth level

This level is about having a sense of order in your life. You may be disorganised, with a tendency to be late for work or social events. You may be known for your untidiness and have a home full of clutter, or perhaps have little interest in doing a good job, thinking you have to do it just to pay the bills. On a more extreme level, there are the rebellious types who believe that society's rules are made to be broken. You always turn up late and leave your home in a mess. You may dress in a non-conformist way and hate the idea of any kind of regular work. Perhaps you judge others who do keep order in their lives, believing that this is for the 'straight people' who don't understand how to be creative and free. Because of this people will feel that you cannot be trusted and that you don't care about their feelings. Although this may seem just a physical manifestation, in fact you will not have a strong sense of purpose or feel that you have a place in the world. Perhaps you believe you are just another cog in the wheel of life and it may be hard for you to see an overall pattern to existence.

As a metaphor for how this sense of order or structure is important in our lives, think of how you feel if you walk into a room full of junk. We all know of a room like this; it might be our spare room, or a room belonging to a friend or relative. It might be full of old clothes, shoes, jewellery, bedding, books, paperwork, boxes, it's no longer a room, just a storage place for clutter. As you walk in you may feel uneasy and constricted. Now imagine seeing the room transformed. There is shelving for the books, a blanket box for bedding, a rail for clothes, a file for paperwork and worthless rubbish has been thrown out. Everything is where it's meant to be and there is a sense of order. You can walk in this room and relax or sit in here if you wish. There is space and you get a sense of freedom and elation from it. Consider how, on many of these home makeover programmes on television, people become emotional and cry at seeing parts of their life in order. These feelings arise because now out of this order, previously trapped energy flows freely again. The sense of ease and excitement from this order stirs our creative force into action.

It is exactly the same with any disarray in life. Order brings boundaries. If you are chaotic and erratic, no one can respond to you properly and you will be seen as a loose cannon.

Perhaps you can now see why having a sense of order in life is essential and allows space for transformation.

30–50 Strong fifth level

This reflects a strong sense of order in your life. You are professional, tidy, punctual and well presented. As a result, people feel they can trust you and know that you won't let them down. Respecting order in your life shows a strong caring attitude, because you are respecting other people's boundaries, time and space as well as your own. Even though you may not consciously realise it you are connected to the greater pattern of life. This enables you to feel fulfilled and part of the greater scheme of things on an unconscious level. People can respond to you and everything functions properly because there is a sense of everything operating as it should.

How to ensure a healthy fifth level

This level becomes weak when we don't address the need for a sense of order in our lives. This can happen to any of us when we become ill, depressed or experience a loss or trauma. When we have a sense of falling apart inside, our outside world reflects that and we simply can't be bothered to care about ourselves, our job or our environment. And when we let the structure of life fall apart, we feel even more lost.

Look at your thought processes in this area. How do you think when it comes to keeping a sense of order in your life? Do you keep things tidy at home? Or do you think, I can't be bothered, or I like things messy? Perhaps you were ordered to do housework by a parent and you feel resentful now you're an adult. How do you feel about working efficiently or turning up on time? Are you deliberately late because you want to do what you want, when you feel like it? Do you want to do the best job you can when you are working? Or do you just skim through it while clock-watching the day away? How about your appearance? Do you take care of yourself and make sure you are clean and well presented or can you not be bothered and just throw on the nearest garment to hand? What about paying bills? Can you find where you put them and do they get paid on time?

These negative attitudes lead to chaos and stress for yourself. Not only do they constantly upset others who will see you as selfish and unreliable but you will always feel like an outsider looking in. Think about the effects your actions have on others and replace the thought with a more positive one. But you will need to be vigilant because these thoughts are hard to change. I will work to the best of my ability, I will keep my home tidy, and I will turn up on time. Then immediately act on them to show that you mean business. This isn't about being a perfectionist or obsessive, but aligning yourself to the order of life. Once you do this you will feel a stronger sense of your place in the world.

When this level is functioning well you experience a powerful sense of completely understanding the purpose and pattern of existence. Suddenly everything makes perfect sense, where you are in your life now and how everything has led you to that moment.

Remember

- Be punctual and reliable.
- Be professional.
- Work diligently.
- Keep your home tidy.
- Take care of your appearance.
- Respect other people's time, space and well-being.

SIXTH LEVEL: Higher Spiritual love

This is the level of higher divine love and reflects our need for many spiritual experiences.

1. ***What are your views on God or spiritual experiences?***

☐ *a) I'm open-minded and interested in developing myself; or I've had a few spiritual/paranormal experiences.*

☐ *b) I'm cynical. People who have so-called spiritual experiences are deluded or living in a fantasy world.*

☐ *c) I have had many spiritual experiences and have often felt inspired and elated by them.*

2. ***Do you meditate:***

☐ *a) I have never meditated. I wouldn't know what to do or be able to sit still long enough.*

☐ *b) I regularly meditate or focus on visualisations.*

☐ *c) I believe meditations and visualisation help and I try to do them when I can.*

3. ***How much spiritual nourishment do you give yourself?***

☐ *a) I often mix with like-minded people from my chosen religion/group to commune and focus on my beliefs; or I regularly take time to sit at peace with myself.*

☐ b) *I have no religious or spiritual beliefs.*

☐ c) *Only very occasionally do I look at the spiritual side of my life and sit and spend time with myself in silence.*

4. ***How connected do you feel to your spirituality?***

☐ a) *I often feel a strong connection with my higher mind and feel inspired and creative. I have amazing prophetic or guided dreams and experience telepathy.*

☐ b) *I'm not aware of feeling anything remotely spiritual.*

☐ c) *I occasionally feel inspired and creative and have the odd dream or instinct about something.*

5. ***How happy do you feel to be alive?***

☐ a) *There are times when I feel miserable because of difficulties, but fleeting moments when I feel great to be alive.*

☐ b) *Sometimes I have hard challenges to face, but I often feel a sense of joy and excitement at being alive.*

☐ c) *I hate my existence. I often feel that life is a struggle and wish there was an easy way out.*

Scoring

1.	a) 5	b) 0	c) 10
2.	a) 0	b) 10	c) 5
3.	a) 10	b) 0	c) 5
4.	a) 10	b) 0	c) 5
5.	a) 5	b) 10	c) 0

Your sixth level explained

0–30: Weak sixth level

A weakness in this level shows that you find it difficult to understand what people mean by 'spiritual experiences'. You may not be open-minded enough to hear this but it shows a lack of spiritual nourishment, which we all need in the same way as we need food. You are not sure whether you believe in a higher power. Perhaps you wonder if God is a fantasy to make people feel better. It is important to strengthen this part of your aura, otherwise you may feel that life is meaningless and that you're part of an ongoing treadmill until you die. Living in a world where there is no faith in a higher power, no higher love guiding you is a cold and desolate existence. But it doesn't have to feel like this. Look at your thoughts with regard to spiritual and paranormal experiences. If you feel cynical try to adopt a more open-minded approach. Read and listen to other people's spiritual experiences. Doing so will touch your heart and inspire you – if you let it – and enable you to feel more connected to a higher reality.

35–50: Strong sixth level

As your level is functioning well, you will be strongly in touch with your spirituality. You may have had many spiritual experiences or regularly meditate and understand what it is to be centred. You will often feel inspired, experiencing spiritual love, elation, joy and bliss. These feelings prompt a sense of expansion and connection: the emotions you have when you are in the countryside and feel connected to the trees and the birds flying in the sky. You understand the idea that we are all one and are comfortable with the knowledge that we are spirits living in a body.

How to ensure a healthy sixth level

We all have times in our lives when we lose our faith in a higher power or feel disheartened. When something terrible happens to someone we love or we experience illness we may wonder if a higher power that we call God really exists.

Begin by looking at your thoughts in this area. What prompts you to want to be at peace with yourself instead of rushing around? What is the meaning to existence? Do you prefer to switch off and live life on automatic, or do you want to discover a deeper connection in your life? Be honest with yourself and if you are thinking, what's the point? turn it around to, I have to know more. A deeper spiritual hunger gnaws at everyone's spirit and is the source of much pain if it is left unnourished. If you don't feel interested in spiritual growth you are blocking yourself and will feel deeply unfulfilled. How do you block yourself? By going into denial? By inappropriate use of drink, drugs or food?

Look at ways to inspire yourself through higher thought. Develop your psychic abilities and work through this book for example, which will enable you to open the door to enlightening experiences. Or simply learn to become more still. Meditating quietly as you concentrate on your breath will soon strengthen your sixth level, as will practising yoga, listening to melodious music, being around nature or taking time to look at a sunset. Seek out like-minded people from your chosen faith, yoga class, meditation group or spiritualist church and inspire each other.

Instead of feeling blinkered and hemmed in by angry or irritating feelings, shift your perspective to the bigger picture of life and everyday problems will no longer seem to be an issue. You can raise your consciousness to a higher level when you feel inspired about life.

Remember

- Practise meditation.
- Listen to melodious music.
- Listen to and share other people's spiritual experiences.
- Develop your intuition.
- Be around nature.

SEVENTH LEVEL: The creative, divine mind

This level concerns our need to be creative and make our highest dreams, ideals and ideas become a reality.

1. ***How creative are you?***

☐ *a) I often come up with creative ideas for my work or in my life and make them work practically.*

☐ *b) I often think creatively but never do anything with my ideas; or I often get creative blocks.*

☐ *c) I'm not interested; or I don't have any creative ability.*

2. ***How strong are your boundaries?***

☐ *a) I occasionally feel vulnerable.*

☐ *b) I feel very spiritually protected as if nothing can harm me even when I am walking alone at night.*

☐ *c) I often feel vulnerable and am nervous of being attacked or hurt.*

3. ***Have you ever experienced telepathy?***

☐ *a) I often connect telepathically with people and sense when they are thinking of me or trying to contact me.*

☐ *b) Telepathy doesn't exist, it is a load of rubbish.*

☐ *c) I have fleetingly experienced a sense of telepathy with other people, like answering a phone call from a friend when I've just been thinking about them.*

4. ***How much do you accept yourself?***

☐ *a) I strive to attain perfection in myself. I don't accept weakness.*

☐ *b) I accept my weaknesses and the fact that I'm not perfect. But I do my best.*

☐ *c) I know I'm not perfect, but I sometimes give myself a hard time wishing I could do better.*

5. ***What do you believe about the universal pattern of life?***

☐ *a) What pattern? I believe that everything is random and chaotic in nature and there is no reason for being here. We live, we die.*

☐ *b) I believe there is a greater pattern to everything but I don't know what part I play in it.*

☐ *c) I believe in the greater pattern to life and the role I play in it.*

Scoring

1.	*a) 10*	*b) 5*	*c) 0*
2.	*a) 5*	*b) 10*	*c) 0*
3.	*a) 10*	*b) 0*	*c) 5*
4.	*a) 0*	*b) 10*	*c) 5*
5.	*a) 0*	*b) 5*	*c) 10*

Your seventh level explained

0–30: Weak seventh level

Life is a creative force and in order to achieve fulfilment we need to feel inspired with an ability to create what we want in our lives. As this level is weak you will probably find it difficult to think creatively or come up with good ideas. You may therefore often feel uninspired, uncreative and unfulfilled. This level also makes us feel spiritually protected and you may feel vulnerable and unsafe at times because you are far too easily affected by other people, because of weak boundaries.

You will also find it hard to understand other people's ideas and broader worldwide concepts, whether they are new medical discoveries, political theories or philosophies. It may even be difficult for you to understand what God means to you and that there is an overall pattern to your life and reason for being here. Consequently you find it hard to accept your imperfections and you may feel uncomfortable in your own skin.

35–50: Strong seventh level

Your seventh level is strong which means you are operating from your creative divine mind. This is the outer level of your aura and extends from your body by about three feet. You feel spiritually protected, which gives you a strong resilient aura with a sense of inner calm and confidence. You have many intuitive flashes, ideas, profound dreams and feel enormously creative. You have the ability to make creative ideas work effectively and other people can learn from them. You may work in the creative industries or as an inventor, scientist, or philosopher. Many producers, writers and artists have a strong seventh level as they take an idea and create something from it that will move and inspire others. The grander the scale of the project, such as a screenplay, movie, philosophical view or scientific research, the stronger their seventh level.

In essence this means you have a strong understanding of God and a sense of the pattern of life and where you fit into it. You accept yourself for who you are but also aspire to something higher. You know your purpose.

How to ensure a strong seventh level

As this is the outer level of our aura, its strength is a reflection of how well our other levels are functioning. It is impossible to have a strong seventh level if the other levels are weak. This level expands the spiritual qualities from our fifth and sixth levels relating to our higher mind. Predominantly, though, it is about the creative divine mind. We all need to trust and develop our creativity and intuition. Society would be much improved if we could tap into these gifts and give full rein to our ideas, inventions and insights, which stem from our creative source.

Focus on the beauty of creativity for inspiration. Go to art galleries, concerts and read books on philosophies. Listen to your dreams and write down what they are telling you. Guidance and inspiration also comes from our dream state when we have shut off our conscious mind and are in touch with higher truth.

To increase the strength of this level practise the exercises in this book and nourish your imagination, which will expand and nurture your higher mind and enable you to connect with your intuition and creativity. When your psychic self comes to the fore, your creativity will flow naturally. When it does, be ready and paint, write or sculpt with passion in your heart and see what evolves from the inner you.

We all have a creative purpose to fulfil in our lives; we just need to discover what it is. Let your inner soul express itself and lead the way. After all, inspiration, intuition, flashes of new concepts and hunches are the source of creativity.

Remember

- Nurture your creativity.
- Turn your ideas into reality.
- Develop your intuition.
- Use your imagination.
- Pay attention to your dreams.
- Walk your talk. Be who you say you are.

Now that you have worked your way through this questionnaire you will have discovered any imbalance within your own mind. You have begun to understand yourself better and in doing so activated a deep cleansing process. This is simply because you have become more aware of any negative thoughts and beliefs that are holding you back, and by replacing them you eliminate the poisonous negativity that keeps you stuck in old reactive patterns. You are in an ideal position to see how you can change your life and improve your relationships by taking responsibility for the way you think. And as you continue to strengthen the levels of your aura you will become the powerful, balanced and intuitive person that you deserve to be. You can then experience a more profound intimacy with your partner without past baggage holding you back. Or your energy will draw you to a more like-minded partner with whom you can connect fully creating a deeper psychic bond.

Next, let's look at the way your mind works in connection with your relationship.

How your beliefs affect your relationship

Do you keep attracting the same type of person? Think of the pattern in any unsatisfactory relationships: is your partner always the dominating type or are they lame ducks who need rescuing? The following thought exercise will tackle your ideal vision for a relationship and the belief that is holding you back. Remember, your beliefs are what you are. Change them and you change what you attract.

The partners you've attracted may come from different backgrounds, have varying careers and look unalike, but their behaviour may none the less be similar. Consider what attracted you to them. On what level did you connect? Think of your mind as a computer where all your thoughts, desires and beliefs are programmed by your experiences of life. Particularly as children our minds were like sponges soaking up all the information around us and that formed our attitudes to life and therefore our behaviour. If we were abandoned, belittled or criticised we believe that to be deserved; and as a consequence, what we believe is what we will attract as our reality. The information remains in our auras and becomes our blueprint for life – until we change it. So if your belief is that you will be treated badly by a partner you will attract someone who will fulfil your expectation.

For example, a girlfriend of mine, Felicity, complained that she always attracted philanderers who never seemed to love her. When she looked at the pattern of similar men, it suddenly dawned on her that her father was a philanderer who never gave her affection, exactly like her ex-husband and all her boyfriends. She realised she had a belief programmed from her childhood that men couldn't be trusted and would never give her the love she needed. Once you discover your own pattern you can begin to change your beliefs. Felicity's thoughts were sending out like-minded signals of what she accepted to be true. Similarly, all your thoughts, from your current attitudes to ingrained beliefs from the past about how to be treated, will attract the same type of person who mirrors who you are or repeats what you expect.

The basis for it could be negativity on the second level concerning feelings towards yourself. If you haven't healed this past experience, it will come back to haunt you in terms of the people you meet as part of your life's healing process. The same type of person will home in on you and you will feel familiar and comfortable with them initially, because you are used to their attitudes and behaviour. But being at home with bad behaviour or negative energy doesn't make it right or healthy.

And therein lies the nub. What you think and believe about yourself or relationships becomes your reality. Make sure the reality is what you want it to be. Write down your thoughts to clarify your understanding of your blueprint. You have the power to change it and take the first steps towards transforming your relationship patterns.

As you continue to develop and strengthen the levels of your aura, you will need to clear out negative beliefs and attitudes constantly. They have been entrenched for a long time, and you need to be vigilant in order to keep your mind clear and positive. Once you change your beliefs about what you expect your thought energy will change and this will affect the dynamic of your relationship, bringing out a more loving response in your partner. Alternatively, if your beliefs are now resonating on a different frequency to your current partner, you may attract a different type of companion. It will take effort, but once you have gained control over the way you think, you will have mastery over the kind of relationships you want.

We will aim to implement this new-found awareness of your thoughts fully through an exercise that will help you transform your beliefs about your relationships.

Transform your relationship patterns

Make two lists: My Vision and My Beliefs. Your vision is what you want to achieve in a partnership and your beliefs are what you expect you will get. This will enable you to see how your beliefs may be holding you back from having what you want. For example, Felicity's vision was that she wanted a generous man who adored her, was good in bed, loyal and dynamic with a good job. The men she attracted had all those qualities apart from much needed loyalty. They were always unfaithful or just didn't seem to fall in love with her. She was the one left wanting more. She needed to change her beliefs about men.

The same applies if you think you've found Mr or Miss Right but the relationship isn't going the way you want. Under your vision write what you ideally want to happen, such as commitment, children, a loving, attentive relationship with your already chosen partner. But if it isn't happening that way then look at your thoughts in this area and write down how you believe things will go. Perhaps you believe Yes, this person is right, but discover your other beliefs are I'm not really good enough, or attractive enough, or we're both too busy. You could even ask yourself honestly: Are *you* ready to commit? Often when things aren't going the way we want it can be a surprise to discover that we don't really want it right now anyway.

If you believe you want a strong commitment, your partner cannot help but respond energetically to you. If they fail to do so, it could be that you are not being honest with yourself as to why you are in the relationship and what you believe you want. Your thoughts have wings. We transmit thoughts every day of our lives. They are living things stored in your auric field and, make no mistake about it, they create an impact. They radiate the energy of our emotions and whatever we focus on, they will travel there instantaneously, even from a great distance. People will unconsciously be affected and influenced by your new beliefs and thought energy. Positive beliefs and expectations will create a burst of positive energy that others cannot help but respond to. By aligning your beliefs with your vision you *will* get results.

You are the creator of your own experience.

You are now aware of how thoughts fundamentally influence the way we feel and what we manifest in our lives. But don't expect this new-found knowledge to be plain sailing. You will be challenged to see things in a new way, to understand the patterns of your previous thoughts and actions and to acknowledge that you might have been on the wrong track. That takes courage, clarity and humility.

Knowing how the power of your thoughts can influence the types of relationships you have is the starting point. You can then transform your current partnership into a deep and powerful psychic connection, or you may discover that this bond isn't constructive and that it is time to move on. Remember, the way we attract people into our lives is not haphazard, the result of some outside force controlling our destiny. Your thoughts are the key to your future happiness. You attract both what you are and what you believe you deserve!

So the buck really does stop with you and it's important that you take time to look at where you are in your life. Take stock of what you have achieved so far. Look over the results from the questionnaire: you are now aware of the way you think, which is the first step in implementing changes. Your thought pattern exercise will help you see where you are in your life and that you are in control of what you think, not a victim of your mind. You have already taken a big step. The truth may shock you, but the reality is that *you* are the creator of your life and only you can orchestrate the kind of loving connections you want to enjoy.

By discovering the seeds that were first planted in your beliefs, wants and desires, you can transform that blueprint into the perfect masterplan. You understand that your aura is a reflection of your mind, and by being aware of your own different levels in your energy field you have taken a step forward into true liberation. You were once a conglomeration of all your childhood beliefs absorbed from past experiences, but now things are different. No one else need ever tell you how to think again. Regardless of what has happened to you in your life, you are in charge of your own mind and destiny and it's time to recognise the power you have to create the life you want.

You have laid the foundations. You will soon discover how to tap in to your intuitive mind and discover the answers that will reveal the magical way in which you and your partner can connect. Then your psychic powers can help you fan the flames of your relationship into the passionate and loving union that you both deserve.

3

WHAT DO YOU WANT FROM A RELATIONSHIP?

AWAKENING YOUR INTUITION TO FIND THE ANSWERS

Somewhere something incredible is waiting to be known.

CARL SAGAN, 1934–96, PROFESSOR OF ASTRONOMY AND SPACE SCIENCES

Now it's time to continue laying the foundations towards creating a loving and powerful bond with your partner. In this important step forward you will begin to strengthen your higher mind as you are introduced to the four fundamental tools that will enable you to awaken your intuitive powers and become a supernatural lover. We often look outside for answers in our quest for solutions, but it is by searching within ourselves that we can find enlightenment. Using the simple yet powerful techniques laid out in this chapter will help you to connect to your psychic self and discover what you really want to achieve in a partnership.

We often let our relationships drift or accept conflicts as a way of life, simply because we never question what it is we want from a partnership. Knowing your goal is essential because you can then begin to work towards it. This sense of 'knowing' is even more powerful when it comes from our intuitive self, simply because this is the part of us that understands our true needs with wisdom, discernment and clarity. Without this inner voice driving us we are led by our limited mind, or ego, that creates self-deception, irrationality or unrealistic demands.

You are now aware from the questionnaire in chapter two that your thoughts, beliefs and feelings send out vibrations reflected in your aura that will influence others. You can continue to replace those old beliefs and thoughts that are holding you back with a positive vision of what you want to achieve. The instant you change the way you think, your positive thoughts will radiate revitalised energy through your aura and you will begin subtly to exert a loving influence on your partner as you prepare the ground for new growth.

But this is just the beginning. By using the magical tools explained in this chapter your higher mind will open up, strengthening your intuitive powers. With this fresh understanding you will be ready to unlock a new doorway in your love life and discover the way you connect with your partner. This connection is the very link which magnetically drew you together, and by the end of this chapter you will discover if your attraction is based on a soul mate or past life connection or whether it's based more on sexual energy or mental rapport. By learning about the unique energy that formed your relationship you can use your inherent intuitive powers to unearth the deeper loving potential between you. In the forthcoming chapters your mind will be primed to focus on your partner as you send out potent psychic energy and begin to transform your relationship into the meaningful loving partnership you both deserve.

How psychic powers will improve your relationships

Let's look at why using your intuitive powers will help you in your relationships. To explain further I will use the analogy of the sea. Like us, the sea has many moods. It can be frightening and wildly unpredictable as waves crash against the beach, or it can be tranquil as the water gently laps on to the shore. Reflect for a moment on what your own inner ocean is like today. Is it calm or crazy? Waves, when they are being stirred up by the weather, can be extremely intense; the same goes for our own waves, whether caused by our insecure or negative thoughts or events in the world around us. But you have a choice. You could allow yourself to be thrown about by the thunderous foam as each wave breaks on to another. However, if you happen to be in a submarine, many fathoms below, you will see a completely different world, in which all is still and calm. Same sea, different depth.

This is what happens when you dive down into your inner well of intuitive wisdom: you remain protected and unaffected by the passing storms. When we allow our intuitive powers to lead us, we are in control of our destiny. Everything becomes more joyful and harmonious simply because we are connected to the voice of our spirit. It is from this centred place that you feel more balanced and objective without stress and negativity obscuring your perception. Getting in touch with our intuitive self creates an altered state which, as mentioned in chapter one, is on the same frequency as a feeling of unconditional love.

This will breed a deeper feeling of empathy and affection as you approach your partner from a place of understanding instead of one of expectation and demand. Your finer qualities of courage, wisdom, creativity and compassion come to the fore as they naturally flow from this inner contentment. You can then see beneath your partner's veneer and respond with honesty and awareness rather than giving knee-jerk reactions. You will feel more in control of your thoughts, instead of allowing them to control you and you will naturally focus on the positive qualities of your partner when you are in tune with yourself. That in turn will influence their response to you as they receive loving waves of energy on a subconscious level.

Telepathy is one of the effects of this intuitive connected feeling you have with a partner and enables you to feel a magical intimacy as you share your own private language that no one else is privy to. This breeds a strong sense of oneness and allows you to unfold different dimensions of your relationship by influencing each other with loving thoughts, as well as becoming more receptive to one another's thought waves from any distance.

Our thoughts are powerful forces of energy. What we focus on is felt by the recipient and will influence the way they think about us. That is why the following techniques to awaken intuition will give you the opportunity to transform your partnership into a loving and harmonious bond. You will create a new pattern not just for you and your partner, but for any future generations.

The four steps to engaging your psychic powers

There are many techniques for developing ourselves psychically, but to awaken your intuition and therefore improve your relationships and become a supernatural lover only four are needed. These are Awareness, Focus, Vision and Trust. We shall now explore each of these, as I explain how you will put all four steps into practice to engage your higher mind.

Step 1: Awareness

This is the first essential step in understanding the power of your mind and becoming aware of your intuitive self. It is simply about being conscious of your own thoughts, feelings and actions and taking responsibility for them. Awareness is understanding the difference between your ego and your intuitive self and how they influence your decisions and behaviour in marked ways. You have already begun this process in the previous chapter by becoming aware of the way in which you think on different levels.

Once you understand the impact your thoughts have on your relationships and your partner then you will see how vital it is to recognise the difference between an intuitive feeling and a limited thought coming from your ego. Such awareness will help turn your relationships around.

A single thought is a potent force, especially when you repeatedly think in the same way. The energy from this thought, particularly if it is of a strong emotion such as love or anger, builds up cumulative effects in your energy field. A thought stems either from your intuition (the voice of your spirit) or from your ego (the projected self). So, as I explained in chapter two, it is our thoughts, however longstanding, that are creating our blueprint for happiness or misery. Now let's discover whether you are thinking from your ego or your intuitive, higher self.

Limited Thoughts

Our limited thoughts stem from our ego and negative beliefs. Our limited mind judges everything including ourselves. It always wants to be in control. You will know if you have lost touch with your true self when you react solely from your ego (lower self) with arrogance, impatience, aggression and sometimes even violence. In this state we create conflict and confusion within our relationships. We lose sight of the feelings of others and want everything on our own terms. That's precisely the reason why relationships flounder: we allow jealousy, anger, fear and controlling behaviour to take over. Despite experiencing a great mutual attraction with someone the 'disconnection' from our true selves leads a partnership to become destructive.

Intuition

Intuitive feelings, on the other hand, well up from your inner voice: your higher self. Or if our minds are open (see Imaginative vision section on page 74) we can be telepathically influenced by our guides and higher angelic forces. I use the word 'feelings' very specifically. It is important to note that intuition and love are not thoughts. Love, intuition and creativity cannot stem from a mental process. It might seem like a thought, because a hunch or a creative idea suddenly appears in your mind, but in fact it stems from your spirit and is filtered through the higher aspects of your mind. Our intuitive self wants the best possible outcome that will benefit everyone.

You will know if you are relating to someone from your higher mind because you will act with discernment, compassion and courage and your relationships will reflect this and be harmonious, joyful and loving. In short, when your intuition is applied to this area of your life it can be nothing less than a success. Your fear flies out of the window and you stop trying to control. Everything flows as it should. As you will have a healthy, glowing aura you will attract a healthy lover or bring out the best in a partner with whom you can share and celebrate your life.

Sometimes, though, this inner wisdom tells you when you simply have to cut ties and walk away from destructive people or situations that aren't helpful or supportive. Obstacles and conflicts may arise in our relationships, as in everyday life, but how you respond is up to you. Whatever your decisions are in life, this connection to the real you wants a win-win outcome that is beneficial to you both. It is for these positive reasons that we should aim to listen to our inner voice if we want our relationships to flourish.

What happens when we don't use our intuition?

Without engaging our intuition we can end up as victims of fate, blaming others for what happens to us as we respond from our ego.

Look back at your emotional history and recall how many times you have allowed your limited thoughts to bring you unhappiness. Endless worry, obsession over details, jealousy, preoccupation with ourselves or others and good old-fashioned fear: these toxic thoughts have the potential to destroy relationships.

When we allow negativity to take control we have disconnected from our intuition – the voice of our true selves. The chaos this causes is manifest all around us with the high rate of divorce, abuse and violence. Relationships turn into a survival of the fittest as we become reactive and defensive to others' behaviour rather than responding from a place of harmony and balance.

It's all too easy to allow our ego to take over and be controlled by negative thoughts when we are affected by stressful circumstances and thus lose sight of our inner voice. So bear in mind that when we think about ourselves or our problems, our mind energy funnels inwards, creating a pressure on our brain and causing tension and, at times, depression. This may explain why many individuals in this state are totally insensitive to the needs of others. They are self-absorbed and their intuition is switched off.

Using Awareness to Take Control

We often accept that our mind dictates to us and that we are unable to stop ourselves from being bombarded with certain thoughts. But you *can* take control of your thoughts, by choosing what you want to focus on, and discover the positive effects you can have on other people and yourself. When you think positively or visualise relaxing images your mind energy expands and reaches out into the universe. As it does so you also release dark streams of negative energy and tension from your aura, which makes you feel uplifted and positive. You are therefore more able to pick up on the thought waves from your partner, because your mind is more open and receptive. In turn, this can only improve your relationship by helping you understand and empathise with your partner and also feel more in tune with them.

Keep examining your beliefs and what you attract into your life and see how you can respond to situations to create harmony. It will take persistence. It took your lifetime to create the negative thoughts and beliefs you have and you will have to keep nudging them back into more positive ones. But when you revolutionise the way you think, you will stop giving knee-jerk reactions and you will start to see dividends in what you attract and evoke in the people around you.

Becoming aware of your intuitive self

We've firmly established, then, that for our own future happiness we need to allow our decisions to be influenced by our intuition and become more conscious of the way in which we think. So now it's time to go within and find the connection with your inner voice. After all, if you can't commune with yourself, how can you hope to communicate in a relationship? We can all remember days when everything flowed effortlessly and we felt good. This happens when we are in sync with our intuitive, creative selves. The following exercise will help you tap in to your intuition so that you are able to make clear, constructive decisions from your higher mind rather than your limited mind. Once you've connected to your intuitive self you'll be able to find out what it is you really want from your relationship and you'll also have achieved the first step in engaging your psychic powers to help you reach your personal goal.

Connect with your inner voice

Take a moment to consider how you feel at this point. Be completely honest. Are you lonely, frustrated or depressed? Or do you feel optimistic and contented? Take a deep breath and relax. Whatever it is you feel, accept it. You don't have to pretend to be happy or fulfilled to get what you want. If you feel bored or irritable then allow yourself to experience it and the feeling will soon shift. You may feel temporarily sad, but it will pass. The most important thing is to take off the mask that says 'everything's okay'. We often wear this to keep up appearances to society. But now simply let that mask go and feel who you are in this moment. You can't take huge steps forward and improve your relationships unless you are honest about your feelings. At this point all your delusions, fantasies and pretences regarding how you feel about yourself and your partner must slip away.

Close your eyes, and get a sense of yourself sinking down to the centre of your being. Focus on your breath as your chest rises and falls. As you look into the darkness, feel that empty blackness all around you, but know that within you is an unlimited timeless space. It may seem empty, but within it is your creative, intuitive self. Imagine travelling inside yourself into the core of who you are. Feel a space in the centre of your chest. This is where your deepest longing resides within your heart; this longing is the intuitive hunger that drives you forward to keep you on the right path. It is a still place, beyond your thoughts, where your inner voice speaks. It is your essence: pure energy that is content just to be. Visualise your essence as a golden core radiating light and pure love.

Sit with this feeling and allow yourself to experience any emotions that rise to the surface, even if these might be frustration or disbelief that anything is happening. Now ask yourself: What do I want from my relationship? Allow your desires to well up from your intuitive self and not from your ego, which is full of materialistic ideas that give only temporary satisfaction. The intuitive part of you is wisdom and love at its purest and knows very well the positive potential of your partner and the kind of relationship that will best serve you. From this space, you can allow your heart to dictate the way forward. This is vitally important, because the more your request comes from the heart, the more likely you are to get what you want. But if you are complacent your vision won't be as potent and the results won't be what you hoped for!

Let your intuition speak to you

Take a moment to see what your intuition has to tell you. You might receive a flash of inspiration or insight about your relationship. Your intuition works in different ways, so you might receive something in the form of a hunch, a strong inspired feeling, or a sudden thought. Write down anything you receive as that will help you to crystallise your feelings. Do you get a feeling of clarity, inspiration, or understanding about what it is you need? Remember, it is what you want from your relationship that is important. For example, your logical mind may tell you that you want more attention or to be complimented more, but your intuition may reveal that you want to exchange and learn more about the qualities and strengths of your partner.

Questions to ask yourself

1. Did you suddenly feel that your relationship is stale or panic that things aren't right? Don't worry. Just accept how you feel. In the forthcoming chapters you will have an opportunity to turn things around, but from a place of honesty not deception. You will be able to see your partnership clearly and whether it is possible to bring out its potential or decide to walk away.
2. If you felt that you had problems feeling anything, that's fine. You may have been unconsciously operating from your limited views for much of your life – perhaps trying to conform and do what society or your parents or partner expected from you. If you haven't focused on your own needs and intuitive feelings before, then give yourself time. You have to begin to get in touch with yourself. Practise listening to your inner voice and follow what you feel, not what you think. But try not to get frustrated or stressed. Intuition flows when we feel relaxed and happy. Aim to have fun. You might, for instance, suddenly get a

flash of insight while watching a comedy on television, or chatting with friends.

You now have a greater insight into the importance of aspiring to remain connected with your intuition. Gaining awareness of how you feel as well as the impact of your thoughts and beliefs mean that you have taken huge steps understanding the language of your psyche. You have opened a door within and located the voice of your own spirit and if you keep listening to this wise part of you it will tell you the truth about what you want in your love life, with no delusions clouding your vision. And as you learn to give that voice attention, it will gradually get louder. You are now well on the way to awakening your psychic potential, so let's move on to step two, which is how to focus the mind.

Step 2: Focus

Focusing your mind is essential to achieve any goal. There is a well-known saying: 'Where your consciousness goes, energy flows', which is so true. When you focus your mind on something, you send energy to it; the more you maintain the focal point, the more energy accumulates. So the next important aspect to cover is to focus your mind on what you want to achieve in your relationship. The more you focus on this the more your vision will create the thought frequencies in your aura to attract it to you. Your thoughts are energy and you will naturally gravitate towards a partner who is like-minded. If you are experiencing conflicts in your relationship or have reached a stalemate, you need only get back to the common denominators that first existed between you.

Focus on what you want

So, you've begun to think about what you want. Okay, hold that thought. If you want to bring out the best in your partnership then you need to focus on the different aspects that you require to make things work. Look at the circumstances of your relationship and write down your answers to the following questions to reflect on later. You might feel you are in a stable relationship, but is your partner married or playing the field? Do you need more loyalty from them or want more of their attention? Focus on the qualities your partner has. Are they dedicated to their job with a stable income? Then start to look at what you want to improve in all areas. Does your sex life need improving and why? Have you or your partner gained weight? What other qualities would you like to enhance in your partner to meet your needs? Should they be more generous, loving or help around the house more?

These aspects of coupledom might seem straightforward, but if things need to be improved in any way, you need to look at those facets of your relationship that work and those that bother you, in order to know how to remedy the situation. I have put together some prompts below, which will help focus your mind. The questions will nudge you into a clearer idea of what you are looking for to get the best out of your partner and what you want to change to improve your relationship. Do note, though, that this is not an exhaustive list: add any topics that relate specifically to you and your partner. Pinpoint those areas that matter to you and write down your thoughts to clarify them in your mind and as a reminder of the direction you wish to take.

- What would make your partner more attractive to you? This might cover different areas: perhaps you'd like them to be slimmer, physically fitter, to eat more healthily, not smoke or drink so much, be more relaxed, chatty, sociable and so on.

- How would you prefer your partner to smell?
- How would you prefer your partner to dress?
- Is your partner single and available to be with you in a relationship?
- Can they spend quality time with you on a regular basis?
- Is your partner fulfilling their potential at work?
- Are they solvent and financially stable?
- Do they have a strong work ethic?
- Do they live in easy reach of you?
- Are they optimistic with a zest for life?
- Do they have a healthy self-esteem?
- Are they mentally stable with a keen intellect?
- Do they have sexual hang-ups or do they enjoy making love?
- Do they treat you with respect and value you?
- Do they share any of your interests?
- Do they compliment you and feel physically attracted to you?
- Are they romantic and do they readily show tenderness and affection?
- Do they allow you the freedom to live out your dreams?
- Are they able to communicate openly and honestly?
- Are they loyal and monogamous?
- Have they moved on from the past by focusing on you and the present?
- Do they have a good sense of humour and do you laugh and have fun together?
- Do they allow you your independence without being possessive and demanding?
- Do they have spiritual beliefs and want to nurture them?
- Do they want children and do you share those thoughts?

As you become clearer as to what you want your list may change. A true partner is a mirror to who you are – so if you want improvement, look at the positive qualities you yourself have. If you don't feel you have many, then perhaps you need to go back to chapter two and do some more work to bring out your own finer qualities and thoughts. The important step forward is to be clear and honest with yourself about what you have and what you want to achieve and not to settle for the same old life if you're not happy. For example, if your partner doesn't care about their appearance and is reactive, stressed out and would prefer to slump in front of the television giving a Neanderthal grunt rather than a proper reply, focus on the positive idea of your partner as a calm, affectionate, attentive lover who cares about their appearance. By constantly creating a positive vision, you are seeing them at their best: happy and fulfilled and therefore able to respond as a loving, caring individual. By focusing your mind in this way, you will affect the way your partner feels on an energy level. They will suddenly be flooded by this positive vision of themselves that you are holding in your mind and start thinking about you in a more constructive way. These new clear thoughts will become part of your auric blueprint and you will find that your positive feelings will make you subtly respond to your partner differently, instead of being miserable or shutting off. In a short period of time, you will steadily start to see the best in your partner, whatever they lack, and they will begin gradually to respond in kind.

Now you have identified the improvements your relationship needs, it is important to remember this: always look behind your thoughts to the underlying belief. For example, if your partner is married and you are embroiled in an affair as the third party, or perhaps you believe your partner is being unfaithful, would you like them to be more committed and loyal to you? If so, you need to look at your beliefs that got you into that relationship. It may be that you are the one who is frightened of being in a committed relationship, or perhaps you don't feel worthy of anything better. It is what drives your thoughts – the belief behind the thought – that you also have to be aware of. By doing so you can change that thought to one that makes you believe you really want commitment.

You have achieved a huge amount already in your psychic development by disciplining your previously untamed mind energy and awakening your intuition. By focusing this vast energy on the task you want to undertake you are now heading in the right direction for the transformation of your relationship. Your mind is primed and refreshed, ready to absorb new information in the same way that you dig over your garden to plant new seeds.

It's now time to give your mind an intensive exercise 'work-out' and take a journey into the realms of your imagination. What you focus on can begin to accumulate power and profoundly influence your partner – simply by creating a vision of what you want.

Step 3: Imaginative Vision

You have become aware of how you feel and uncovered a deep inner space that enabled you to connect with the voice of your spirit. To implement this further and channel your intuitive forces so that you can influence your life, you need to expand your higher mind through creative visualisation. This is where imagination comes into play.

Visualising what you want is the foundation to any success in your life and is one of the most important elements of your psychic development. It is a crucial bridge that you need to cross to reach a heightened state of consciousness that will accelerate your psychic powers. You should never underestimate its potency to influence anything you focus on. This is because it provides a solid focal point that creates sensations in your body and emotions. So what you imagine becomes a real experience that influences you. This inner movie screen is so versatile that you can evoke any kind of feeling by using it. You only have to picture your favourite meal and your mouth will water. Or remember a passionate encounter and your heart will race. So imagine how powerful it could be if you use it as a tool to relax into a more peaceful state and expand your mind so you can more readily listen and act on your inner voice.

Your imagination is a conduit for all expression – creativity, vision, dreams – and by using it you also open up a channel for other beneficial influences to filter through. Higher beings such as guides and angels are always around us, and they can make an impact on you when you enter into an altered state of consciousness. This can happen when you meditate, dream or visualise and they make their influence felt in your hunches, insights and inspiration. As a consequence they also enhance your intuitive powers and help you resolve problems or create coincidences.

The benefits of visualisation are immense on every level, physical, psychological and spiritual. As visual imagery raises your mind consciousness to a higher level you become deeply relaxed and calm. This releases accumulated tension from your aura and you may feel slightly light-headed. Try out one of my visualisation exercises whenever you feel stressed, or have a conflict that you need to resolve. Whenever you take time to do these visualisations your mind energy will expand outwards into the universe and you become gradually more open and receptive, developing a higher extra-sensory awareness. This enables you both to listen to your inner voice as well as to empathise more deeply with the people in your life.

Your intuition will continue to grow ever stronger when you use your imaginative skills, as this faculty strengthens and exercises the intuitive and creative side of your mind. Imaginative visualising is therefore the main ingredient to the exercises as you develop your intuitive skills, but through the exercise that follows you will also develop the vision of what you want to achieve. Prepare to exercise your imagination, expand your mind and begin developing your intuitive powers . . .

Taking a journey into mind expansion

Before you embark on any of the visualisation exercises find a quiet space where you can relax and be alone. Any room where you will be undisturbed will do. Take the phone off the hook and create an ambience that will help you to relax. Play soothing, melodic background music, light some candles and some incense if you wish. Make sure you are wearing comfortable clothes and that the room is the right temperature for you.

Try to visualise your imaginative scenarios as clearly as possible, paying attention to the detail of the picture, but also to the sounds and sensations you have. If your re-creation is as realistic as it can be, this will strengthen your imaginative skills even more. All the exercises will make full use of your imagination and help you focus your mind. Not only will your mind energy open up which, as I explained, enables you to connect with your intuition, but also in the forthcoming chapters your mind will be primed to focus on your partner as you send them potent psychic energy, the aim being that you will connect with their higher mind. This fresh intuitive energy enables you to feel more connected with each other and will filter through to your emotions and physicality, influencing all levels of your relationship from your communication to your responses to any obstacles.

If you find it difficult to recall what I've said from the written word, record your voice reading the different exercises. Then you can play back the visualisation while you are relaxing. But if you do so, speak clearly and at an even pace so that you don't hinder your concentration.

You are now going to expand your mind energy and enter into an altered state by going on a journey to engage the imagination and thereby heighten your vibrational frequency. This will release stress, limber up your mind and enable you to be more receptive.

Engage your imagination and connect with your higher mind

Imagine you are walking across a lush green field. It is a summer's day and you can feel the warmth of the sun on your skin. You take a deep breath in and smell the sweetness of freshly cut grass. All around you can see the green of the field for miles like an emerald blanket shimmering in the sunlight. The combination of the green with the azure blue of the sky makes you very calm and relaxed. As you walk across the field you can feel the grass beneath your bare feet and you can sense a gentle, refreshing breeze. Then suddenly in the distance you see a hot-air balloon. You walk towards it wondering if it's really there or just an illusion. As you get closer you realise it does exist when you see a large basket and a huge balloon made from gold and blue material. The flames are underneath, already fired up, ready for the balloon to fly. You walk over and climb inside the basket.

Once there, you see how large the basket is and how big the balloon is above your head. The balloon starts to take off and you feel it slowly sway as it rises up smoothly and you hold on to the sides. As it ascends you feel comfortable and this seems like the most natural thing in the world to be doing.

As the balloon goes further into the sky, you look at the blue all around you. Looking down, all the trees look like tiny specks and the fields blur into a coloured map. The houses all around the surrounding area quickly blend into different-coloured roof shapes. You can now see clouds around you, of varying shapes and sizes. As they float along, you feel lighter and the air seems cleaner and fresher as you see the sun shimmering from the clear sky above the clouds. You feel the balloon gently bobbing across the blueness but continuing to rise higher as everything on earth now seems to be a distant memory. You have risen so high that the clouds are now below you and you take in a deep breath as you feel enveloped in the blue sky all around you. Then you suddenly feel a sense of the balloon beginning to descend slowly. As it gradually moves back down, you see the different shapes of clouds again. Then the map of coloured fields and houses comes back into view. And before you know it you see the expanse of vivid emerald-green fields just below as the balloon slowly and gently lands back where you started. As the balloon finally settles into place, you climb out and sit on the grass, feeling its crisp texture beneath you.

Questions to ask yourself

1. Did you find it easy to visualise? If not, don't worry. It is just as valuable to get a sense or sound of the scenario, even if you can't picture it clearly.
2. Did you feel safe in the balloon as it rose into the sky? If not, persevere until you do. It is important to feel safe

with your own imaginary powers. The more you get used to using your mind in this way, the more comfortable you will be about visualising yourself in different scenarios.

You have limbered and toned your higher mind and by doing so you have also opened up your mind energy and begun to awaken your intuition. This has laid the foundations for the exercises you will do in your relationship, in the same way as you need to warm up before you embark on any vigorous exercise programme.

Create your vision

Next you will use your imagination to create a vision of what you want to achieve. As you have already discovered in chapter two we often unconsciously create a vision of life from our beliefs that have been input from our experiences. So creating visions of what you want to achieve in your love life is a real role reversal. When you were a child your mind was a clean slate ready to absorb information, and it is our beliefs from our closest relatives and childhood experiences that lay down our attitudes and feelings about life. In this way our minds become programmed and if the input was adversely negative we can become fuelled emotionally by this energy, which affects how we feel and respond to events. If we believe, for example, that we are destined to fail or that all relationships are fiery, we will attract and create that reality. As I mentioned earlier, this can shut us off to our higher intuitive minds as the negative thoughts and feelings make our mind energy funnel inwards, leading to depression or hostile feelings. Now you have the opportunity to take control of your mind, and re-input the positive information you want. As we have found out, when your intuition starts to flow you are led by your inner voice which helps you make wise, loving choices. Once you begin to listen to this more you will no longer habitually respond from the knee-jerk reactions of bitter or miserable experiences.

You have already focused on what you are looking for. This has given your mind a goal to aim for and you will start to create new thoughts and beliefs about this outcome. Visualisation is now the next step to solidify what you want and make your ideal a reality.

Make your dream a reality

Write down a detailed description of everything you have focused on – in the present tense. There is an important reason for using the present tense. Our unconscious higher mind does not understand the past or future. It only understands the reality of something as happening *now*, which is why recalling a traumatic event means you relive it. Of course, you immediately feel depressed and this instantly affects your auric field. Likewise, seeing your vision in the present means you begin to experience it. This recharges your aura creating new, positive thought forms. And this affects your energy and your behaviour for the better.

Writing down what you want sharpens your thoughts and focuses your mind to make your vision more of a reality as you subconsciously begin to see it as a belief. For example, 'I am enjoying a loving and secure relationship with Steve. He is being very generous and supportive towards me.'

Once you've written your description, begin to visualise your current partner spending time with you in a romantic scenario.

This is a creative visualisation not a fantasy, so keep your mental picture based on the reality of your lifestyle, choosing the peaceful surroundings of your home or a restaurant rather than an imaginary beach in Barbados. Make your visual picture as detailed as possible, so that it engages all the senses as I described in the previous visualisation exercise.

Begin by focusing on how relaxed you are feeling. What are your surroundings and where are you sitting? Is there music in the background? Consider how you are both dressed and what you can smell. What kind of conversation are you having? Is it animated and intimate? As you are picturing the scene, say an affirmation in your mind, which confirms the picture; for example, 'We are loving and honest with each other.'

Do this type of visualisation and affirmation for half an hour every evening and morning for several weeks. If you change the scenario then you may manifest the situation in a different place. So if you want intimacy to happen more at home, or if you wish your partner to take you out to dinner more, keep recreating this background and add that to the affirmation.

It takes a while to change your beliefs but your mind will quickly respond to repeated visions and thought patterns and with regularity it will accept it as a real experience that is already happening. You will create deeper intimacy with a loved one or be mutually attracted to someone you may never have noticed before who is on your wavelength.

Once you have created your vision you have amplified your psychic powers and they will begin to manifest themselves in your life. On an energy level miracles are already working on many levels of your mind. Just like your thoughts and feelings, this concentrated picture will exist in the layers of your auric energy field and radiate a new vibration. Remember that we all pick up information psychically from someone's aura and instinctively know if we gel with them or not. Similarly the person in your vision will be affected by this powerful energy that is happening in the *now*. Thoughts travel and your partner will sense and respond to them even from a distance. They will suddenly get a warm burst of energy and find that they can't stop thinking about you or suddenly get a spontaneous urge to spend quality time with you, take you to dinner or buy you flowers – whatever you keep imagining.

On a psychic level, positive visualisations are powerful and give you a highly charged feeling of knowingness and expectancy, expanding your mind energy, releasing tension and plugging you into a deeper communion with your intuitive self. Your own sixth sense will be sharpened and you will be more receptive to your lover's thoughts and feelings which will help you feel more in tune. Instead of believing that your relationship isn't working, that you might argue over money, children or ignore each other and watch television, everything has changed. What you believe is now stemming from an inner vision, emblazoned with all your senses. You believe that your relationship is blossoming, that you will spend loving and intimate quality time together and that you feel secure and open with each other. And your new heightened intuition, optimism and energised aura will send out potent magnetic vibes that will penetrate deep into the heart and mind of your partner. And they will begin unconsciously to respond to your vision.

Now you are empowered and a creator of your new life, you are ready to move on to the fourth step of psychic awareness: trust.

Step 4: Trust

Trust is vitally important. It is about relinquishing control and insecurity and being open, accepting and yielding as a young child in need of help. Imagine the universe as your ultimate parent who can give you whatever you want if you trust that this gift will be given to you at the right time. You can't be impatient or stamp your feet and make demands, you must simply yield to the fact that it will happen.

Trust takes belief to the highest level; it is not just about having confidence and being optimistic. Without trust, none of the other psychic development tools will work! You need to trust absolutely that your relationship will improve and that your intuitive techniques will fulfil their purpose. The alternative to trust is to feel fear, insecurity and negativity. When they occur we block our intuitive powers and feelings of genuine love from flowing, and trust flies out of the window. Our progress is then stunted as we get caught up in the agony and misery of our limited minds.

When we trust in our own intuitive power we become more confident and our psychic powers grow stronger. This is important, as many things that we respond to intuitively often make no logical sense. Let's face it, falling in love isn't logical or convenient, but we know that it feels real and meaningful when it happens.

So although focusing your mind and using your imagination will have powerful results, you must let go of the outcome and trust that your psychic abilities will produce the effects you desire. If you keep thinking about achieving the right outcome or get impatient, you will exhaust yourself mentally and create stress – which is the opposite of the relaxed state needed for you to tune in to your inner voice.

Whatever your circumstances, know that your every need is completely provided for if you can only relinquish control and in doing so allow this higher supportive force to take over. When you do this, there is no fear or worry. You don't feel the need to control the outcome. And when we absolutely 'know' that the universe will provide everything we need – that alone can create miracles.

Susie's story: Having faith in trust

Susie was twenty-five and lived in a small, quiet village in Yorkshire. She worked for herself as an artist but she was in a rut and nothing in her life was going right. She was single and work had dried up. She decided that she needed a fresh start and thought about moving to London. She felt intuitively that by being in the capital she would be at the hub of things, make more business contacts and get out of her rut.

She was worried that she didn't know anyone in London and didn't have much money to put down on a deposit on a rented flat with city prices, but decided to rent out her one-bedroom flat in Yorkshire. Her friends and family were against her going and kept bombarding her with all the obstacles that she might encounter. But Susie had faith in her decision and decided that she would implicitly trust that she could quickly create a successful life hundreds of miles away. She found lodgers within weeks of advertising her flat, but also met someone else who had phoned about it, with whom she immediately struck up a rapport. When she told them she was moving to London, they immediately gave her a phone number for a relative who was looking for someone to rent his two-bedroom house.

She headed down to London to look at the house and discovered the rent was easily affordable. As she left the house, she got talking to her new neighbours and was invited to a dinner party the next night. Coincidentally they knew someone who had opened an art gallery who was looking to display some new artists' work. One year on Susie is dating the gallery owner and planning to get married. Despite moving to a new area and not knowing where she would find work or a social life, Susie proved that by completely trusting that everything would work out for her – it did. She had a new home, new friends and new business contacts within a few weeks. Her trust in a higher energy took care of her, helping her intuitively to bump into the right people at the right time.

Trust is essential to our psychic powers, because the more we trust that everything will be taken care of, the less we fret and try to control the outcome. As a consequence the stronger our psychic sixth sense becomes; it creates the right coincidences that support us in our endeavours. Whether it's a situation in our lives or solving a conflict in a relationship, trusting that we are using our intuition and are on the right pathway will work miracles.

Discover Your Connection

You are now equipped with the foundation knowledge of your psychic proficiency as a supernatural lover. Having been introduced to the four crucial psychic tools, your higher mind has been awakened and your intuitive abilities primed. You also have a clear vision of what you want from your relationship so it's time to move forward and use these techniques to revolutionise your love life. In doing so you will continue to develop and strengthen your inner powers as you focus your mind to bring out the deepest loving potential within your partnership.

But before you begin using your psychic powers to work their magic, you first need to discover the way in which you magnetically connect with your partner. It might be as a soul mate, through a past life link, a mental rapport or pure sexual attraction. I have devised a quiz that will enable you to see clearly the specific way in which you and your partner were first attracted to each other. So, however your relationship is now, you will be able to focus on the common denominator(s) that brought you together.

Your Magnetic Attraction Revealed

Here we come to the crux of this book: a series of questions that will provide you with the compass points you need to direct you forward. The answers will lead you to the chapters that will illuminate the essence of your relationship along with psychic exercises that will reawaken and strengthen the love between you. This is what you have been working towards.

By understanding the nature of your own mind in chapter two, with its thoughts and beliefs, you have become aware of the impact the energy of your thoughts has on yourself and others, reflected in your auric field. You know that thinking negatively influences an outcome. You can't have a successful relationship if you are reacting to present circumstances from low self-esteem, or old childhood wounds. Aiming to use your intuition creates more positive, loving thoughts as they stem from our inner feelings and send out uplifting energy that boosts the person our mind is focused on. This is why taking conscious control of your thoughts is one of the most empowering skills a psychic can develop.

This self-awareness was the cleansing process needed before you moved on to discover the four principles of your psychic awareness earlier in this chapter, so that you can understand the way in which your psychic energy will be exercised and focused. With your consciousness now heightened you will be ready to use aspects of these four techniques in the different exercises designed to bring out the potential of your unique magnetism with your partner. Discovering the basis of the underlying attraction of your relationship is the starting point to unearthing how you became a couple. By doing this you will be going back to your roots, the intuitive drive that drew you together, before your limited mind created problems.

The questions to which you answer yes will simply reveal the way you connected. This may be in more than one way. For example, you could discover that you have a past life as well as a soul mate link. The quiz will also reveal the problems that have caused disruption to your relationship. Simply circle any yes answers and check them with the scores at the end.

Discover your magical connection. *A questionnaire to reveal the very essence of your partnership.*

1. *Did you get an instant attraction and feeling of familiarity when you first met?* *Yes/No*
2. *Did the relationship start on a basis of friendship?* *Yes/No*
3. *Do you think a strong sexual attraction is the only thing you really have in common?* *Yes/No*
4. *Did you experience telepathy and/or psychic experiences initially or since being together?* *Yes/No*

5. *Are there many things you wish you could change about your partner?* Yes/No
6. *Do you have unresolved resentment towards your partner?* Yes/No
7. *Do you find the way your partner thinks a turn-on?* Yes/No
8. *Is there real unconditional love generated between you?* Yes/No
9. *Did you click on a mainly intellectual level?* Yes/No
10. *Did you feel as if you connected on many different levels?* Yes/No
11. *Do you feel that you drifted together and that there has never been much common ground with your partner?* Yes/No
12. *Did you have an overpowering longing after you met to see your partner again?* Yes/No
13. *Were you drawn together by your mutual interests and enjoyed exchanging different ideas?* Yes/No
14. *Would you describe the chemistry between you as an animal attraction?* Yes/No
15. *Does your partner frequently press your reactive buttons, making you feel hostile or defensive?* Yes/No
16. *Do you feel bored and unfulfilled with your partner?* Yes/No
17. *If you had to go without sex for months because of ill health, would your relationship quickly end?* Yes/No
18. *Do you have joint goals and feel a sense of respect and compassion towards each other?* Yes/No

19. *Do you sometimes feel you are strangers to one another?* Yes/No
20. *Have you ever had a dream or a sense of knowing your partner from another time or country?* Yes/No
21. *Is the underlying reason why you stay with your partner based on convenience or finances?* Yes/No
22. *Did you feel compelled to become intimate with your partner as soon as you met?* Yes/No
23. *Was there a powerful feeling of energy between you when you first met?* Yes/No
24. *Are you frightened of your partner?* Yes/No
25. *Did you get together out of mutual loneliness?* Yes/No
26. *Did you feel a deep emotional connection to your partner from the first few times you met or communicated?* Yes/No
27. *Are you deeply unhappy in your relationship most of the time?* Yes/No
28. *Is sex the most important aspect to your relationship?* Yes/No
29. *Is your partnership based on a strong attraction that quickly turned into destructive conflicts?* Yes/No
30. *Do you think you are better friends than lovers and/or the friendship will remain after the passion has diminished?* Yes/No

Scores

Now check how many 'yes' answers you have circled under each of the six 'links' below, and note which link holds the majority.

Soul Mate Link

Q4, Q8, Q12, Q18, Q23: turn to page 93.

Past Life Link

Q1, Q10, Q15, Q20, Q26: turn to page 135.

Primal Link

Q3, Q14, Q17, Q22, Q28: turn to page 179.

Mind-to-Mind

Q2, Q7, Q9, Q13, Q30: turn to page 215.

Destructive

Q5, Q6, Q24, Q27, Q29

Disconnection

Q11, Q16, Q19, Q21, Q25

Where do you go from here?

The quiz has illuminated the essence of your relationship by focusing on the different auric levels that connect you with your partner, as well as any destructive tendencies. Having circled your answers under each of the link sections, note that the one with the most yes answers is the main link on which you and your partner connect. Turn to the appropriate chapter relating to that link, which will explain the nature of your relationship further and help you improve this quality with psychic techniques. If you have two links with many yes answers then you are operating on two main connections, so both chapters for these would apply.

Also note any yes answers to any destructive elements that have crept into your relationship. These are the issues that you need to improve on by using your psychic energy. For example, if the quiz reveals you have a strong past life link, but it has become destructive, then you need to reignite the positive energy that once existed between you. Equally, you may have a partnership that is based solely on a friendship link, but because there is no deeper connection, during any conflict you might feel as if you are two complete strangers. If you have more than one yes answer in the disconnection section then I'm sure you already know that there is no real kinship in the way you and your partner think and feel and therefore little opportunity for growth. However, you can still use some of the psychic exercises to try and discover yourselves more and you may find that you do indeed share some common ground.

Perhaps you have a cross-section of yes answers which doesn't highlight any particular link. If so, you may not be focusing on the questions properly. Go back and redo the quiz, concentrating on what the question is asking and how it applies to your relationship.

But be aware that you might discover that the basis of your relationship might be quite different from what you thought when you look at your circumstances in depth. For example, you might believe your relationship has become so destructive that the original link was just a tentative friendship, when in fact it was a past life link. Often past life connections can become stained with bad karmic issues from your history that need to be resolved. In this case the psychic energies will benefit you enormously as you reawaken the deeper aspects of your love.

A note on the exercises

The psychic exercises throughout this book can be used by everyone to improve their partnerships; however, each of the following chapters will use specific psychic techniques which are especially applicable to the connection you have.

You can develop your strengths and learn how to heal any destructive issues or damaging patterns within your relationship and focus on building a powerful intuitive bond that will take you to new heights. Once you have finished with the pertinent chapter, you can ask your intuition to guide you to the next exercise that would be useful to you. A tip is simply to close the book, focus your mind as you visualise flying up into the sky and sitting on a cloud and then open the book at the page you are drawn to. Then see which exercise jumps out at you.

This thorough preparation of the four techniques will have paved the way for working magic on your relationship with a clear, focused and awakened higher mind. Now that you have the key to the way you and your partner magnetically connect you are finally ready to breathe new life into your relationship. So get ready for a transformational adventure!

THE SOUL MATE CONNECTION

A RELATIONSHIP BUILT ON A JOINT SPIRITUAL DESTINY

Every artist dips his brush into his own soul and paints his own nature into his pictures.

HENRY WARD BEECHER, 1813–87, WRITER, LECTURER AND REFORMER

In this chapter we will look at one of the most powerful and sacred of the four connections that we will explore in this book; the soul mate link. Make no mistake about it, this is a special attraction, connecting you on all levels of your aura, as your like-minded energy creates a magnetic empathy. This connection is unique because at the core of this relationship is a spiritual destiny, which you share.

You can discover more about why you were drawn into this intense attraction, what happens when a soul mate relationship goes wrong and examine how to overcome the heartbreak and moral dilemmas posed if either of you were with someone else when your paths crossed. But just as importantly you'll soon see why it's so essential to understand the higher purpose to your partnership and begin to work towards your joint spiritual goals.

Having discovered the strengths and weaknesses within your relationship from the questionnaire in chapter three, through specific exercises you will soon put into practice the four techniques, and focus your mind to harness the powers of your imagination, creativity and dreams to heal any conflicts and strengthen the bond between you by developing and channelling your psychic energy. Through trust and confidence in your innate powers you will then steadily build on the intuitive sixth sense that already flows between you. With your magical union you can create a powerful allegiance that has a higher purpose with far-reaching results.

What is a Soul Mate?

A soul mate is someone with whom we share an intensely powerful attraction. These individuals are a counterpart to our mind energy, connecting with us on all levels, so you will instinctively sense that you are mentally, physically and spiritually in tune as soon as you meet them.

Contrary to belief, there is no such thing as 'the one', meaning only one person with whom we are destined to experience true love. Each of us has several soul mates whom we may meet during our lifetime and to whom we could be attracted in a non-sexual way, such as a friend or a relative; they belong to our soul group. We learn spiritual lessons from our group members and we feel drawn to them, as they share the same quality of mind energy and are therefore our most like-minded allies.

But take note: your soul mate may not be the adorable angel you imagine. They could be an irritating, loud-mouthed character whom you dislike, yet you may still feel drawn to them by a powerful attraction, in spite of their failings. It is your deeply emotional feelings that will tell you the truth about the nature of the relationship.

A soul mate is one of your most ancient friends whom you may have reincarnated with repeatedly, although a soul mate can act as a guide (someone who can help us evolve spiritually and understand more about ourselves) whom we have never known in the physical state. But we know them from our time between our physical lives when we were pure soul essence and we can often meet up in our dream state when we sleep.

However, here we are focusing on our physical life where there are different types of soul mates, who can also be known as your other half, a twin soul or essence counterpart. These soul mates can be the companion or lover who helps you reach your spiritual goal, or a karmic teacher (this could be a friend, a short-lived affair or a one-off meeting) who comes into your life for a short time to teach you an important lesson or support you in reaching your spiritual goal. Your spiritual goal is what you are being propelled towards: a joint spiritual destiny, unique to soul mates that you are destined to embark on together. This could be working towards your highest aspirations and may involve healing or teaching. So even if a soul mate relationship doesn't run smoothly there are always spiritual lesson or strengths to be gained from the encounter.

Your Soul Mate

If you have discovered you have a soul mate bond then you will completely understand the feeling of incredible energy that flows between you and your partner; and perhaps you have already shared some profound psychic and spiritual experiences. You will have known the moment you met your soul mate, because they woke you up to your very core, in a way no one else had ever done before. It is a deep emotional bond that instantly connects you and defies all reason.

Whatever your individual circumstances, one thing is for sure: the union brings a fast track to spiritual learning and there is often a much higher purpose to the union than simply playing happy families. I say this because it is so important to clear up some of the clichés about soul mates; don't assume it is a problem-free relationship for life.

We all have a perfect blueprint for our relationships, which we discover when we follow the voice of our intuitive selves. As with all partnerships the freedom of choice as to how you react to circumstances lies in both your and your partner's hands – and therefore so does the outcome. With this type of spiritual energy, a soul mate will often appear in your life at a time that you might find challenging or inconvenient, or you may undergo difficult circumstances together. The success of your relationship depends on how you both handle the connection between you and stay in touch with your higher self.

To give more clarity on the energy connection of a soul mate relationship, let's first look at a positive example of soul mate energy. In the following example, the two partners endured challenges within their relationship, but worked towards supporting each other.

Fiona's story: achieving happiness

Fiona, thirty-seven, is married to Neil, thirty-nine, and they have three children, but during their marriage they have both experienced many challenges as Fiona suffered six miscarriages. A feeling of powerful energy drew them to each other from the moment they first met at their local gym. Fiona says, 'I remember walking reticently into this room with muscular men pumping iron, but in the midst of them was Neil and I immediately felt as if

I knew him. It was as if his presence filled the room. Everyone else seemed to fade away into the background and left just the two of us. I didn't think, Wow, this is the man I'm going to marry, it was stranger than that. I actually felt as if we were already married and had just been separated for a while.

'I walked over to him almost speechless. He smiled at me, but didn't give anything away as to how he felt. I can't even remember what I said next. I was just lost in the moment.

'We both made chit-chat hesitantly at first, and at the end of the session I offered him a lift to the station. For the next two months we continued to meet at the gym twice a week. We swapped work numbers but we never went for a drink or discussed anything personal. We both kept our cards close to our chest.

'Although I often wondered if he found me attractive, he was like an iceman as far as me being able to detect any flicker of emotion from him. But every time I saw him, our future together seemed to become more of a reality.

'It wasn't just a feeling of chemistry or physical attraction, it was a sense of feeling right, as if we completely belonged together. I had never felt anything like it before. I didn't want to suggest meeting up socially, because my emotions were running high whenever I saw him and I was wary of revealing my feelings, which seemed too powerful to voice. I was scared that he might not feel the same as me.

'But a few months later, everything crystallised. Neil went to Germany on holiday and I missed him desperately. I realised I must finally tell him how I felt: I didn't want to continue without him in my life.

'Coincidentally, just as I was feeling this sense of urgency, he called me from Germany. "How are you?" he asked. With that I just poured out how I felt. "Well, actually, I really miss you," I heard myself say, my voice shaking with nerves.

'My heart was pounding, I didn't know how he'd react but he said instantly, "That's exactly what I've been waiting to hear. I'll be home tomorrow."

'When I met him from Heathrow he said, "I knew from the word go that you were the woman who would have my children but I didn't know how you felt." Within a month we moved in together.

'There also seemed to be a real psychic link between us and Neil suddenly announced one day, "We'll have three girls called Frankie, Georgie and Charlie." Remarkably that prophecy eventually came true. But for the first few years of marriage I suffered three miscarriages and would cry myself to sleep wondering if I would ever have children. I remember Neil walking into the bedroom and saying, "I know you've lost our babies. But I've also lost my wife and we need to work through this together." I realised then that I was isolating myself through my own misery instead of recognising that we both had needs.

'Many years later we now have three healthy daughters: Francesca, seven, Georgina, six and Charlotte, three. But during that time I also suffered another three miscarriages. Neil is incredibly positive and he has taught me that we never know what tomorrow brings, so we need to focus on today and appreciate what we have. Sometimes with all the problems I've had in the past, I can't believe how lucky I am to have children. Now when they are asleep I often go up their room and look at them and feel happy for the very fact that my children are alive.

'Neil and I both feel very connected and support each other when we feel down. Now we have such a strong bond we often pick up on how we are both feeling, even from a distance. It really is a feeling of harmony and oneness that I'd never known before. After ten years together I still feel very blessed.'

As you can see from this case study, no relationship is immune to challenging circumstances or negativity, even one that is based on a deeper soul connection. These disheartening and traumatic miscarriages might have split up some couples if they had focused on the negative side. But remaining positive and looking for the best in each other has kept Fiona and Neil's relationship strong.

On a psychic level, remaining positive is crucial to staying connected to your intuition as it keeps your mind energy expanding outwards, which releases tension and enables you to empathise with your partner more fully. This is because you are more receptive and open to the nuances of what your partner is feeling. Taking time to focus on your partner's finer qualities means you intuitively see their spirit, not just their character flaws.

If you allow yourself to give in to stress your mind funnels inwards and you disconnect from your inner voice, which leads to selfish reactions as our focus shifts to our own misery. Remind each other to stay positive and look for the good in each other so that you can overcome the obstacles of life and the weaknesses in each other's character.

Your Soul Mate Potential

When your relationship is functioning constructively you and your partner will bring out the best in each other. When your relationship works well this fulfils another agenda too, as it reminds you of your highest spiritual goals because your partner is destined to fulfil the same potential. These spiritual goals are your compass in life and when you are guided by your intuition you will discover that missing piece of the jigsaw that makes you feel 'fired up' at fulfilling an inner purpose to which you feel drawn. In the latter part of this chapter you will be able to uncover exactly what that purpose might be.

Remember this: the soul mate energy is unique. At your very best you are lovers, teachers and guides to each other. You are there to experience unconditional love, discover your limitless potential and help each other to grow spiritually. At times you may have to look beneath the surface and not get distracted by petty disagreements, but focus on the positive qualities that you admire in your partner and take note of what you feel, rather than what you think.

Now let's concentrate on the weaknesses in your relationship that the questionnaire may have highlighted. You were asked some specific questions on how you felt about your partner or certain aspects of your relationship. If you had more than one answer in the destructive category then there is evidence of detrimental elements creeping into your relationship. This is your opportunity to discover what you can do to resolve matters.

Destructive Tendencies

If you discovered that the questionnaire revealed a weakness in your relationship that could prove problematic, this chapter will help you to focus on using your psychic powers to bring out the enormous potential in your relationship. Your response to those specific questions revealed issues that have arisen between you, which you were probably already aware of by the way you feel towards your partner and how you react to each other. If you feel demoralised, uneasy, or that communication between you isn't honest you will have known there was a problem, but perhaps pushed it to the back of your mind.

Whatever your circumstances are now, don't worry. It is possible for soul mates to find a way back to each other as you have so much to gain, but only if you are both willing to allow yourselves to focus once more on the positive aspects of that incredible energy link that exists between you.

Feelings of Disconnection

If the questionnaire revealed a lack of kinship between you at times, then there could be several reasons for this. First, it may be that you don't have a soul mate link at all. Perhaps you were not entirely honest in your answers. Many people like to believe they have a soul mate bond when they have spent years with a partner, when in truth they don't. Soul mates are always brought together by a powerful palpable force that cannot be ignored, and with a genuine soul mate bond, even if you experience conflicts, you will still feel a strong unconditional love for your partner. This is quite different from two people who simply find each other attractive in various ways, either on a physical level and/or through a strong mental rapport. Take another look at your relationship and note that if you are with someone who is violent, aggressive or controlling then they are certainly *not* your soul mate. Even if your partner doesn't display such extreme destructive tendencies, it is none the less all too easy to project an idealised vision on to them.

Answer the questions again, being searingly honest with yourself about how you felt at first meeting and how you feel now. If revising the questions confirms that a soul mate connection is now not so obvious, turn to the chapter that reflects your new answers. However, if your answers still indicate a soul mate connection, yet you sometimes feel as if you are disconnected strangers, then clearly you have both lost your way in the relationship. Your hearts brought you together, but you have allowed your limited minds and egos to focus on the negative aspects.

There are often hurdles to overcome when you meet a soul mate. It is not always plain sailing. But true soul mates have a joint vision. If this is the case, you now have a choice. The exercises work very effectively but only if you take a leap of faith and trust that they will help you refocus on the positive qualities you both have. Or perhaps you both need to face up to the fact that you have to move on and discover what you need in your life right now. This chapter will help to connect you with your intuition and guide you in making the right choices.

It is important to consider, although often frightening for those who resist change, that sometimes we need to take our courage in both hands and move on from a relationship that isn't working. Before we explore how to heal our relationships let's look at when and why it can be crucial for both of you to go your separate ways.

Knowing when it's time to move on

It's time to leave if the relationship is stuck and neither of you is prepared to work at putting in the required positive energy and effort. The psychic exercises throughout this book demand both perseverance and trust in order to see results. If you feel lethargic or you are simply not interested in working things out then you need to question whether it is worth staying in a relationship that makes you feel that way.

When we act from our intuitive self our soul essence shines through our personalities and we act with kindness and compassion. But when our limited minds take over we make judgements about everything, including ourselves, and we focus on all the things that are wrong about a person and the relationship. However connected you are on a soul level, if you or your partner cannot act from your true nature you will not serve yourselves or the relationship. In this case you may both have lost your focus for what your hearts intended. Remember that all the work you have done so far is about being true to yourself and therefore aspiring towards a more fulfilled relationship with yourself as well as your partner. Partnerships that reach stalemate or have too many unresolved issues or conflicts can become neurotic and unhealthy and can block both of you from moving forward constructively. In turn this stops you from growing emotionally and spiritually. Only you can know the answer whether to persevere or move on. Continue to develop your intuition and you will clarify your feelings and perhaps discover there is another plan for your life with a partner who is more suited to bringing out your positive potential.

On the other hand, now that you have honestly considered the weaknesses in your relationship you may decide to commit to developing your union and reconnecting with the deep love that exists between you. If so, then the pages that follow will help you to understand the soul mate bond further and will show you practical ways to engage your intuitive powers to create a deeper and more loving connection with your partner. You will also discover how to link with your joint higher goal in which your spiritual destiny is for ever intertwined.

Understanding and Healing Your Soul Mate Connection

At this point we come to the first of the specially formulated exercises that will engage the intuitive powers of your mind. Each mind adventure in this chapter employs the second and third techniques of focusing the mind and using imaginative vision in different ways. The exercises are progressively geared first to cleanse you both of negative issues, then to take you to a higher level of your mind and help you to create a deeper psychic bond with yourself and each other, awakening feelings of unconditional love. The final exercises on creativity and dreams will enable you to develop your intuitive powers further and build on the psychic bond between you.

Make no mistake about it, these imaginative focusing tools will have a huge impact on you and your partner. Any concerns you have about your relationship, whether boredom, hostility or fear, will evaporate as you stimulate your own intuitive powers, which evoke a higher vibrational force creating inner harmony and contentment. This state is allied to loving unconditionally and ultimately affects the way in which you respond and react to your partner (as discussed in depth in chapter three). Those with a genuine soul mate link always have a strong psychic bond and often experience telepathy, as they are so like-minded. But issues that arise within a partnership or the pressures of everyday life may have blocked that flow of intuitive feeling.

The following exercise is an important starting point as it will expand your higher mind, release tension and negative energies. This is essential to cleanse your energy field of any stressful issues which, once released, will facilitate a flow of energy, so that you are ready to move on to the next exercise and connect to your partner feeling relaxed and open. You will then have cleared your own energy field and prepared yourself and your partner to reconnect.

Flowing with the tide

Picture yourself and your partner sitting next to each other on a secluded golden beach in the late afternoon. It is a perfect time of day as you can still feel the warmth of the sun's rays but there is a pleasant breeze. You can feel the warmth of the sand beneath you as you sit facing the azure blue of the sea watching the waves ebb and flow. Your eyes are drawn to the glistening water as the sunlight seems to sparkle, dancing on the surface. Become aware of your tranquil mood on this beach and see how the calming blue of the sea seems to merge with the sapphire-blue sky. There isn't a cloud in sight. Take in a deep breath and sense how your skin seems to be drinking in the vibration of this colour. Now feel the presence of your partner next to you. You can see their profile as they stare out at the horizon. See how peaceful their expression is and how their chest rises and falls with every breath. Whatever kind of day you have had all your stress and tension seem to melt away as you gaze at the deep blue ocean without a care in the world. As you breathe in again, you can smell the salty air and every now and then you hear the sound of seagulls as they fly overhead.

Now watch the waves again as they slowly ebb and flow into the shore. Sense the awesome power and mystery in this magnificent ocean. Remember the magnetic power in the tides that is so strongly linked to the waxing and waning of the moon. Keep watching the waves gently lapping into the shore and feel how calm it is now, but bear in mind the potential of the wave and how it can suddenly become so much bigger, stronger and more magnetic.

Feel how strongly your spirit and energy are attuned to this mysterious ocean. Sense the connection and how something deep within you resonates with the immense primitive force of nature. Now be aware of the connection with your partner and the sea. Sense how the force of the sea and both your spirits feel attuned to each other and at one.

This time as you watch the wave flowing into the shore, I want you to inhale deeply and hold your breath, until the wave slowly ebbs out. Focus on your breath and the waves three more times. As the wave rolls into the shore, inhale deeply and wait for a few seconds, breathing out as the wave recedes. Note any stress or tension in your aura. You can visualise it as dark streams of energy. Get a sense of the weight this negative energy carries. It could be in your shoulders weighing you down or the heaviness of tension across your brow. Now wait again as the wave flows into the shore; as the wave recedes sense its powerful magnetic force and visualise it tugging on your energy field, pulling away any stress and tension that you have accumulated in your aura from any area that you feel needs to be released. You feel much lighter and cleaner. As the wave continues to recede into the vast blue ocean, know that the negative vibrations are being carried far away and will be transformed and evaporated into the universe by the rays of the sun. Know that this same process is happening with your partner.

Now sense any unresolved issues that are blocking your relationship with your partner, whether sexual, spiritual or emotional. Or they might simply be symptoms of pressures that you have had to face together, be it financial, emotional or ill health. Whatever these issues are, they are just dark streams of negative energy that block the flow between you and your inner voices. Dwelling on the negativity has only created barriers; now it is time to let them go and refocus on the love you share. This time feel the wave tugging at both your energy fields as it ebbs away. Visualise all the dark energy being pulled away from both of you as if a magnetic force is jointly drawing it out and carrying it away to the depths of the ocean to be transmuted once again by the sun. You should feel much lighter and closer to your partner as the heaviness of all your negativity has been washed away.

Now imagine turning towards each other and visualise your aura expanding, getting bigger and bigger until your energy touches your partner. Feel it swamp your partner with healing energy. You can sense this force as white or golden. Now visualise that your soul mate is extending their aura towards you. Sense what it's like to feel their positive clear energy. What feelings do you have as their energy flows over you? Sense their wisdom, loving nature and honesty. This is their real spirit shining out. Then extend your energy again to them and feel the energy between you merging as you both extend your auras towards each other. Stay in this feeling and then pull your energy back towards you.

After this exercise you should feel exhilarated, cleansed and much more in sync with your other half. Your intuition will be heightened as you have not only exercised your higher mind, but also released any negative thoughts between you and created positive healing energy. Visualise in this way whenever you have a problem; the more you do, the more you will keep your thoughts positive and productive. After each visualisation you will sense yourselves being healed and connected together in essence, reminding you of the love you share and your joint soul mission.

Questions to ask yourself

1. Did you find it easy to visualise the waves and control them? If not, don't worry, keep practising. You may need repeated visualisations to learn to control the pictures you conjure up. The ocean is symbolic of powerful psychic and unconscious forces and difficulty in this visualisation may be a sign that you have some resistance to harnessing the powerful forces within you.
2. Did you find it easy to visualise your partner? It doesn't matter if you don't get a strong impression of them

physically, simply knowing they are there and getting a sense of them is enough.

3. Did you find it difficult to allow the waves to take away your negative stress? Keep practising and it will become easier with time. This could also be a sign of your resistance to letting go and trusting the higher part of you to take over.

You have connected with your intuition more fully and washed away any old issues and tensions between you and your partner. This exercise can be a huge catalyst for change and long-repressed emotions may rise to the surface and you might feel tearful or angry. If so, don't concern yourself; these feelings were blocked and are simply surfacing to be released. Sense them wash over you, which will bring you to a point of clarity with your partner. It is essential to focus on clearing away the problems first in order to release negative energy and expand your mind. It is all too easy to let things come between you, whether financial or emotional stresses. Now you have new ground to build on and washing away these negative feelings must be an ongoing process if you want your relationship to succeed.

This exercise proves that you don't have to let the burdens and tension of everyday life get the better of you. Within half an hour you can clear away this negativity and feel a sense of clarity and uplift so that you see each other with a fresh perspective. Without eliminating this cumulative build-up of tension, problems, however seemingly insignificant, have the power to rock the foundations of a soul mate relationship. Read what happened when a couple who were deeply in love with a strong soul mate bond allowed their problems to overwhelm them, which resulted in them leading separate lives.

Anne's story: the break-up

Anne was thirty and worked as an artist when she met her soul mate Richard, a therapist. She says, 'I never had a proper relationship until I met Richard. Looking back it was as if life was on hold until I met him. Every previous encounter with a man always seemed to be blocked. There may have been some chemistry but there was always something missing. Richard was totally different and everything fell into place when I met him at a health fair where I was displaying my artwork.

'Before I even looked at him properly I felt an incredible surge of energy that hit me as he walked into the room. My first thought was, Wow, that's someone really special.

'The display tables were arranged in a circle and as he began setting up his stand to practise shiatsu, a form of Japanese massage, we ended up sitting next to each other and instantly started chatting. When the end of the day came I didn't want to say goodbye. If I could have walked out of the room with him there and then, I would have done. But I thought he was unavailable. He was working with another girl and I assumed she was his girlfriend. Just before he left he took my hand and kissed it. He said later that it was because he wanted me to remember him.

'After that first meeting we didn't see each other again for three months! Thoughts of him would creep into my mind, but I tried not to think about him as it made me feel sad that I might not see him again. Then I was asked by the organisers to another health fair in Blackheath, south London. I didn't know Richard was going to be there but discovered later that the fair was actually near where he lived.

'It proved an incredibly difficult journey for me. I had lots of artwork to carry and several lifts that were arranged for me fell through. I was so fed up that I nearly didn't go, but somehow I had the strongest feeling that I had to get there – even if I had to walk.

Fortunately, at the last minute I got a lift. I felt frazzled and stressed out by the journey but as soon as I arrived, I saw Richard again and in that moment I just knew that I loved him.

'It might seem strange but it felt so right. I walked up to him and he looked really pleased to see me. We immediately hugged each other, but instead of pulling away, we didn't let go.

'Time seemed to stand still. I was desperate to speak to him properly but we had to break away, as people kept appearing to ask me about my paintings. The day seemed to fly by as I was incredibly busy with endless customers, and then, all of a sudden, Richard plonked himself down in a chair in front of me. He said it was the only way we could talk. He asked me if I was okay and then suddenly he said, "I'm falling in love with you." I was ecstatic at hearing his words but totally shocked at the same time. I still didn't quite believe he was single. All I could say was; "You can't be. Are you sure?"

'At the end of the fair we resolved to meet soon and exchanged addresses.It was at our next meeting that we really talked properly. It was only our third meeting in four months. I then found out, much to my relief that not only was he single, but he'd been alone for eight years. We were both overjoyed. We thought that we'd never be apart again.'

This should have had a happy ending. For five and a half years this couple lived together and shared everything. They were business partners with the same hopes, dreams and ambitions. They both felt they were soul partners in the truest sense. But then they split up. Why did such an incredible soul mate link end in disaster? Anne continues the story.

'Things went wrong when we both spent a lot of time building up our own counselling practice. We had no money and tried to keep the business afloat under constant pressure. Consequently, like many people with financial problems, we ended up feeling

stressed and arguing all the time. Things came to a head and Richard misunderstood and thought that I was only interested in work. But in truth, I was simply defending the business because our relationship depended on having stability in our lives. Looking back, I can see now that neither of us stopped and examined what it was we both wanted. I was more passionate about the business than he was. We didn't have a joint vision and consequently it just didn't flow. If we had both remained more honest and tuned in to each other's needs, we could have stayed together but worked on our own separate careers.

'We are still very good friends and speak every few weeks, but I very much regret our parting. The connection never goes. And deep down I hope we may get back together at some time in the future. Even if I married someone else, I will always have this unconditional love for him. He's still in my life as a friend and I can't ever imagine losing contact with him.'

You can see how a soul mate relationship isn't immune to conflict. Despite having a head start over other people, with such a strong emotional bond you can still lose sight of the love you have for each other and destroy your partnership. Anne now wishes with hindsight that she had done things differently and has realised the hard way that the outcome of a relationship depends on each of you. Fortunately, by using your intuitive powers you don't have to let your relationship flounder and break up like Anne and Richard did, only to live with regrets. However your relationship is now, you can practise an exercise to reconnect and refocus on the positive love between you, strengthen your bond and use your own mind magic to turn your relationship around.

Strengthening your connection

In this exercise you will engage your imagination to focus on your relationship bonds. We all have cords of light that bind us together from chakra to chakra. Some of these cords may be unhealthy depending on the way we relate in that area; for example, angry communication will affect the throat chakra and be revealed in discoloured cords. However, if you have a healthy and loving sexual relationship, the cords in the splenic chakras may reveal pure, clear light reflecting the positive aspect of your partnership. By creating a powerful vision of luminous cords of light connecting you both from all your energy points, you will send clear psychic energy into those areas to feel literally more bonded together. Focused mind energy using this specific visualisation will immediately affect you and your partner and profoundly improve the quality of your relationship, enabling you to have more honest communication, greater trust and a more powerful feeling of intuitive synergy, which in turn will lead to deeper intimacy and understanding. For further information on chakras, refer to chapter six, page 182.

Sit quietly and begin by becoming aware of your breathing. Feel the rise and fall of your breath as you inhale and exhale. Don't try and force your breath, just relax. Listen to the sound of your heart. Feel its gentle beat in your chest. Feel a sense of where you are in the room and the space around you. This exercise will work whether your partner wants to join in or whether you are working on your relationship alone. If they are participating, then sit facing each other. If they are absent for whatever reason, you can visualise them sitting in front of you. Take time to do this, seeing them exactly as they might be dressed.

Now I want you to focus on each of your chakra points, visual-

ising the cords of light that connect you to your partner. If you need to, refer back to chapter two to remind you of the location of each chakra. Start with the base chakra. Visualise a cord of light flowing out from your chakra and also from your partner's chakra. See the cord extend and connect with your partner's chakra. Feel the cords of light energy flowing between you, bonding together. Take a few minutes to get a sense of what this feels like. When you make a connection between your base chakra and your partner's base chakra, you will feel more security within your relationship as well as an intensification of passion between you.

As you go along each chakra, if there is any resistance to your chakras connecting, don't worry, just move on to the next one and I will explain afterwards. Keep visualising the connection from your base chakra and now imagine the light energy radiating out from your splenic chakra. Imagine a cord coming from your partner's chakra linking up with yours. Feel the light pulsating as it connects you and once again sense what this feels like for you. Connecting the splenic chakras between you heightens sexual pleasure and desire and increases creativity.

Continue doing the same visualisation with the solar plexus chakra and the heart chakra. A connection from the solar plexus chakra increases empathy and vitality, while heart chakra connections will strengthen your sense of self-worth and encourage a strong emotional bond. *At each point, experience how the light connection feels once it radiates out from you both and connects. Remember that all these connections should remain in place. Now move up to the throat chakra and then the brow chakra. Feel the flow of energy and visualise the light cords connecting you. Throat chakra connections create more honest communication and help you to resolve problems. A connection between your brow chakras will increase your intuitive understanding of your partner. Lastly visualise the crown chakra and see the cords connecting from the top of your head across to your partner's. This chakra connection will expand your consciousness and bring about a feeling of unity and a sense of 'becoming one'.*

Spend a few moments feeling the connection and look at the complete vision. You are sitting opposite your partner with cords of white light connecting each other's seven chakras. Take a deep breath and sense what it feels like. Are you feeling more connected to your partner? Do you get a sense of elation or peaceful energy? Is there a sense of a deeper intimacy as the energy flows between you? Are you feeling more positive within yourself? If not, then don't worry, just know that you have made an energy connection. Even if your partner is absent they will still feel the impact of your positive thought energy.

This visualisation has very powerful results and you may feel a little light-headed or perhaps want to be quiet and reflective, because you have focused strong positive energy towards your partner. Bear in mind that our thought energy vibrates at different frequencies and this exercise has raised your consciousness to a higher vibration. It may take time to adjust, but you soon will once you are more accustomed to using positive visualisation techniques.

As you have taken time to connect with your partner on an energy level your relationship will strengthen and you will feel more tuned in to each other. This will have a knock-on effect as you will find yourself responding to each other in a more loving way without even realising it. Any time you feel negative towards your partner and forget why you chose to be with one another, visualise these cords of light in your mind linking you together. Your vision will enable you to feel more positive and help you to see your partner as they really are instead of focusing on their weaknesses or problems. And because of the energy flow between you, you will experience more of your natural telepathy.

Factors to consider

If there are any chakras that you find hard to connect with your partner, address your intuitive self and ask what is stopping the energy from flowing here. Listen to the immediate answer that comes to mind. You may even see a symbol of what that relationship means, as you would in a dream. Think of the resistance that is happening with a particular chakra. If it's the splenic centre (second chakra), it could be you have sexual problems or if it's the solar plexus chakra (third chakra) perhaps you are having emotional difficulties and not communicating honestly. Don't worry about trying to connect with that chakra for the moment. Instead come back to this exercise another time.

For now sit quietly, place your hands over this chakra and visualise healing energy flooding into it. Whatever happens, don't judge yourself. The important thing always to remember is that we connect better with our partners when we are connecting better with ourselves. Be patient. There is no rush. It is better to correct the area where there are issues or conflicts than to continue trying to visualise all the cords flowing.

Trusting the process

Once you have looked at the way you connect to your partner you will find that you feel closer. Don't try and analyse this. Intuition is not a mental process, and our minds cannot be trusted to tell us the non-judgemental truth. It is how you feel about someone that reveals what they mean to you. Such is the strength of focusing your mind energy in this way that the visualisation is powerful even if your partner doesn't know you are doing it. This is where you need to employ the fourth psychic technique of trust. You have already achieved real magic by focusing your intuitive powers on your relationship in this way. By implicitly trusting that the mind exercises will do their work you are allowing everything to unfold naturally so your psychic powers can do their work. This means you must relinquish control of the outcome between you and your partner regardless of the problems you have experienced and put aside all feelings of impatience, demands or panic. Then you will begin to feel more in tune with each other and the flow of loving energy between you will grow stronger.

You have come a long way in evolving your psychic powers after implementing all four techniques. You have cleared away the tension and negativity from your aura that was blocking your progress and you have reconnected on a powerful psychic level through your chakras.

You have already sown the seeds for a new way of relating towards your partner, but you need to continue to develop your psychic powers and improve your relationship on a deeper level. Using your intuitive powers and developing your relationship in different ways is essential, as the higher mind needs to be constantly surprised and stimulated.

Using Creativity to tune in to your partner

Another way to heighten your intuition is by developing one of your finer qualities that needs to be nurtured continually – your creativity. You'll soon discover why making use of your artistic flair is so important for you and your relationship. Having soul mate energy means you should usually feel in sync with your partner until problems arise that cause barriers between you. Creativity is an important ingredient to develop with a soul mate as it strengthens your psychic energy on all levels, expanding your mind and creating a greater feeling of intuitive empathy.

You will recall that the seventh level of our aura is the level of the creative divine mind (see chapter two). When two people with strong creative minds come together, telepathy is as easy as breathing in and out. This is because both creativity and intuition stem from connecting to our inner voice where inspiration, hunches and flashes of ideas come from. Creating something, whether painting, sculpting, or experimenting with cooking, strengthens that connection between our intuitive self and our conscious mind. When creativity flows, our sixth sense also flows. It is an expression of the real you. And the more you uncover who you are, the more creative you feel. If you are not doing artistic work as a career or hobby then find some quality time to nurture this creative force within you. You can begin by simply writing down your feelings, or you could attend a pottery class or get spontaneous with some coloured paints. Encourage your partner to do the same.

The following creative exercise will help you to develop your psychic powers, further heighten your awareness and strengthen the bond with your partner. It is an exercise in intuitive painting which will enable you to capture and tune in to your partner's inner essence and in doing so tune in to your own. But don't worry about whether you have any creative talent or whether the result will look a mess; the point is to uncover your intuitive connection with your partner and see each other as you really are. The focus is to paint what you feel, as much as what you see. You will need some paper and watercolour paints.

Intuitive painting

If you are working on this exercise with your partner, take it in turns to paint each other. If you want to improve or deepen your relationship without your partner knowing or being present, simply paint their face from a photograph or memory.

Start by focusing on your partner's face. Concentrate first on their eyes and begin to paint an outline. Look at the expression in their eyes and whether it is melancholy or happy. What else do you see about their features? What is the set of their face and what feeling do you get as you paint their nose and mouth? What do you sense as you paint their finer qualities? Are they generous, considerate, loving? Try not to analyse or judge them on the basis of personality alone. If you have experienced any problems, this may be difficult, but look behind the façade and feel what their spirit is telling you. This is where their intuitive voice lies and it knows only the positive. Whatever problems have occurred or negative character traits, this is where the limited mind and ego have overshadowed the finer aspects of the true self. Focus on that energy and ask yourself what the feeling that emanates from them tells you about them. It may be that you are drawn to their ears because they seem to stand out. Does that tell you how much they listen? Study the shadows on their face and see what else shines through from the depths of their being. You are capturing their soul, not just their physicality, so it doesn't matter if the end result is not an accurate resemblance.

The colours you use may reveal much more. Bright vibrant shades like orange and yellow will reveal the vibrancy of their personality, blues and greens will show their healing qualities, pink will pick up on how loving they are, whereas dark, gloomy shades, may show areas of depression, conflict or stress. But once again, concentrate on the bright shades that show the positive aspects of your partner. Just like a flower that is given water, focusing on these and responding to them in a loving way will make them grow and blossom.

This exercise is a way of helping you to use your creative intuitive powers to expand your mind and see your partner in their true glory. Focusing on the positive nature of your partner isn't about deluding yourself, but about seeing them as they are with acceptance and love.

Keep up your creative work so that you continue to develop your intuition and see with the eyes of a psychic. You will feel more fulfilled as a person and if you strive to see this aspect of your partner, positive feelings will only grow, flooding out any negativity. Creativity is another link in the chain to develop a psychic soul mate bond that is deeper and more powerful than you could ever have hoped for.

Practise all these exercises once a week or more often if you feel inclined and your psychic powers will quickly become stronger and this higher energy frequency will keep reawakening the vibration of unconditional love. It will soon become automatic for you to focus your mind on the positive energy between you which will lead to deeper empathy.

Discover the underlying purpose to the Soul Mate Connection

So far you have been travelling on a journey to understand the nature of your soul mate connection. You now know how to heal and strengthen your relationship using specific techniques as well as how to tune in psychically to the essence of your partner. But there is a crucial aspect to this spiritual bonding that no other connection has: a unique spiritual destiny. Soul mates are magnetically drawn together through the core of their beings to undergo an intense learning in which they awaken and support each other whether – and here is the key – they remain a couple or not. With soul mates you will always be invisibly connected to explore your mutual goals even without the physicality of your union. Later on we will explore what your goal is and how you discover it. But first let's examine the extensive learning we undergo from a soul mate meeting.

What we learn from a soul mate

You have read about two soul mate relationships, the happy and the sad endings – and how they help us to evolve into our true nature if we stay connected to our intuitive selves. The dilemma, though, is when a soul mate appears in our lives at the most inconvenient of times, where there are obstacles or other partnerships that block you from being together. This can be confusing and distressing when the energy evoked in a soul mate meeting is so overwhelmingly powerful.

But it's important to realise that every soul mate, behind their mask, is a wise teacher who can help guide you to the right pathway. This is when your soul partner is acting in accordance with your deeper spiritual longing and helping to guide you towards your joint spiritual goals. We often miss what this type of relationship is teaching us when we lose sight of our intuitive urges, but when we learn to see the bigger picture we can understand that separation from a soul mate doesn't mean that we stop experiencing our mutual spiritual assignation. Physical time and space does not stop you uniting on a deeper level as our higher minds and souls are universely linked and can connect from any distance.

The next story about Maggie explores what happened when

she met her soul mate at the wrong time; and how she finally realised twenty-five years later that it was the energy he had triggered in her that would prompt her to look within and connect with her own spiritual destiny.

Maggie's story: bad timing

Maggie, now fifty-five and single, met her soul mate when she was twenty-four. Unfortunately she had only recently married her husband when he turned up in her life.

She was moving house and Terry was one of the group of friends who came along to help. She said that as soon as she saw him she thought he was incredibly handsome. But it wasn't just his looks that affected her. She felt as if she had been hit by an overpowering force that left her feeling dizzy. 'I realised straight away that there was an emotional connection between us,' she says. After that first occasion they kept bumping into each other and each time she had this incredible sense of belonging with him. 'It sounds corny,' says Maggie, 'but it really felt as if I'd always known him. Being with him felt incredibly comfortable. We laughed at the same things and talked easily. But I never expressed any of my feelings to him and we were never alone together. Suddenly after six months he asked if he could meet me alone to talk. I knew he'd eventually say something, as the feelings between us were too strong to ignore.

'I agreed to meet him for lunch, feeling nervous and excited. There was a part of me that wanted to spend that time alone with him, but I was also being practical, considering that I was married and lunching with another man. But I agreed to hear him out at least.

'As we ate he explained how strong his feelings were and said that we couldn't ignore them any longer and how he wanted to spend the rest of his life with me. We talked about the amazing

connection between us and I said, "We've missed each other in time," but I was steadfast in my loyalty and refused to leave my husband despite the unusual intensity of my feelings.'

That was to be the beginning of an ongoing relationship that extended over more than twenty-five years, with what she describes as the deepest feelings she had ever known. However, they didn't become involved physically for another two decades.

She continues, 'Perhaps Terry felt hurt, for soon after that meeting he moved away. Although we had hardly spoken, I missed him desperately. A part of me felt like something inside had been severed. But time ticked by and dulled the sense of loss, until three years on we met again – only this time he was with his new bride! When I met them together I had no feelings of animosity or jealousy at his new-found happiness. I knew he was too handsome not to meet someone wonderful.

'But on that same night his brother led me to the garden with the excuse of wanting to have a talk. That was when I found Terry waiting behind a tree holding out his arms to hug me – and for the first time I walked straight into them. We kissed and touched as if we'd known each other for a hundred years, and again I felt an overwhelming sense of homecoming.

'It was a rather unusual situation but we sat under the tree and talked for a while. We realised that even though we were both married we still felt a sense of belonging to each other. We discussed the irony of fate and how our paths kept crossing.

'During that time I'd had two children with my husband but we eventually divorced out of mutual incompatibility. Terry was to have four children in his marriage.

'Years later when I became single again I contacted Terry. The longing in my heart to be with him never went. But he was still married. When he finally divorced years later and contacted me, I was involved with someone else. All this time we exchanged

Christmas cards and there was the occasional phone call but our strong feelings for each other always remained.

'After knowing each other for what seemed like an eternity we were finally free at the same time.

'One autumn day in 1985 nearly twenty years after we first met, I had a call from him out of the blue. He asked if I'd married again, and if I were free, would I like to spend some time with him, as he was now single?

'I was in England and he had recently moved to South Africa for work, but I didn't need to be asked again. I was on the next plane, thrilled to be seeing him again.

'We spent an amazing two months together. It was pure perfection: a spiritual, physical, mental and emotional bonding that allowed me to feel totally at peace with myself and everything around me. It was like a piece of the jigsaw puzzle had finally been found.

'However, our union couldn't last. There were complications with us living in different countries. I was happy in Britain and he didn't want to leave South Africa. So we decided to part company. The situation was too complicated with work and family and it was heartbreaking.

'He visited me here on and off and thankfully we managed to transform the relationship back into a friendship, which is how it remains today.

But the emotional connection is still there and always will be.

'I admit sometimes I do look back and think of what might have been. We could have spent many fulfilled years together, instead of the endless longing for each other that we both went through. But I chose the moral decision.

'Although we both tried to make it work there were always obstacles in the way, yet I can never forget him. We are two parts of the same whole but instead of endlessly yearning for him, I

finally realised that if I experienced that profound love with my soul mate, that love also existed within me. I learned to meditate and began to pay attention to my intuition. I finally felt inspired to become a counsellor helping others and realised that I felt fulfilled with or without my soul mate. I had found my true goal. What was amazing is that a few days after this realisation I had a phone call from Terry, saying that he had suddenly felt that he needed to change the path he was on by helping others. It was almost like we were both working together towards a joint destiny even though we didn't have an ongoing physical relationship. I am grateful to him for triggering that awakening and we will always remain connected. He has taught me a lot about the invincibility and longevity of soul mate energy. In reality, I spent less than three months over two decades with my soul mate and yet the energy feeling between us lasted longer than with any other lover.'

What Maggie's story tells us is that our future choices are in our own hands, but it may be crucial to the spiritual development of you both that you experience only a short liaison or friendship. If you have ever felt blocked from being permanently with someone you felt to be your soul mate, know that this remarkable force that you experienced reveals a connection that will never disappear whether you remain together or not. Soul mate meetings occur because of a much higher game plan than your conscious mind is aware of. But the feelings of overpowering love ignite your intuition and awaken you to a deeper part of yourself. You then kick off the process towards discovering your spiritual goal.

So what is your goal?

Every human being has a spiritual goal. But with a soul mate the difference is that you and your partner share a common spiritual destiny, which is the underlying purpose of the compulsion that drew you together. You don't discover your goal so much as connect with it. It is your intuitive knowledge deep within that stirs you, inspires you, and moves you emotionally arousing your desire to teach, create and heal. Your aspirations and feelings of being 'fired up' by something act as a compass to your goal. These feelings keep pointing the way. Often our spiritual goals are simple to attain if you are in tune with your higher intuitive self. For example, if a woman is easy-going and enjoys being a loving wife and mother, has no worldly ambitions yet is kind and generous, she is acting in accordance with her goal – which is to heal. For others, reaching your goal may mean that there are many obstacles to overcome and many qualities to gain in order to achieve mastery of your destiny.

On a grander scale, you only have to look at the life of Diana, Princess of Wales, with all the intrigues and insecurity that plagued her, and yet it was her spiritual goal of healing that shone through; one of compassion and the gift of empathising with others. It is this goal for which she has long been remembered and which caused such a mass outpouring of grief when she died.

With soul mates that goal is a joint mission. When we find out what it is we feel fired up, we know our place in the world and have a sense of being on the right path. Reaching your goal is the realisation of all your many lifetimes and you experience a sense of joy and purpose. You may know your goal already or perhaps you are still trying to find it.

When you make a life together with a soul partner, you are

aspiring towards a joint destiny whether you know it or not. However, you only sense your joint goal if you follow the voice of your intuition and this keeps your relationship on track.

Even if you meet a soul mate who enters your life for only a short time, the goal still exists for both of you. This is because you are two parts of a whole, so when you follow your true calling your soul mate will be influenced wherever they are in the world by your energy. And you in turn will be affected by their heightened consciousness. As soul mates' mind energy is of the same quality, you will feel this more powerfully and it may come as a sudden sense of joy, fulfilment, realisation or understanding.

By connecting to your higher mind and using your intuition every day you become more in contact with your final goal. And, remember, your soul mate is there to help you connect with this. When you learn to connect with your intuition more fully and focus on the deeper aspects of your union, everything between you will blossom and fall into place. If you have separated then you can still ask in your mind for their support and their higher energy will flow towards you.

Now we turn to the value of your dreams and how to use them to connect with your mutual goal. Dreams are an important arena for meeting up with our soul mates in spirit form and through them you can work together to discover your joint purpose. Or if you have already found your goal you can use your dreams to allow it to flourish. For soul mates it is a fulfilling way of working on your spiritual growth together. (You can do this whether you have remained with your soul mate or are now on separate paths.) It is only by finding our true goals, what our hearts want us to do, that we find the fulfilment we yearn for.

Discover your mutual goals in your dreams

Dreaming provides essential nourishment for our souls as well as healing our emotions and physical body and gives us a springboard into the higher realms of the mind. Although our bodies rest, our spirits are awake and ready to learn. The dreams that you embark on together as soul mates have heightened benefits if you focus on the higher aspects of your relationship. The energy that flows between you is extremely powerful and you were drawn together to work towards a higher purpose. Your intuition already knows this purpose. It is what your heart longs for you to do. Our dreams are powerful vehicles for learning and it is possible to find the answers to everything in the vast universe within. But before we talk about discovering or developing your highest aspirations, which is your intuitive barometer guiding you to fulfil your goal, there is some preparation to be done so that you understand the value of dreams and how best to remember and make use of them.

The Value of Dreams

Dreams are a form of imaginative visualisation and provide us with a bridge into our intuitive selves. They can be used in many ways: to reconcile your differences, find solutions to problems and communicate higher truths. Dreams are a powerful source of communication and knowledge given to us directly from our souls. The more we tap in to our intuition the more our dreams can reveal guidance and information in a straightforward way. Complicated coded symbols are simply a sign that we are blocking the truth that our soul is trying to convey to our conscious mind.

As you have been developing your psychic powers and building on the psychic link with your partner, this is the perfect time to begin your dream exploits. Keeping in touch with your inner voice is just like giving focused attention to a good friend or lover. The more interest you show in investing in your intuitive relationship, the more the relationship will blossom. And once that inner voice, which has been ignored for so long, receives acknowledgement it will speak to you even louder. Then your inner wisdom, guidance and compassion will come to the fore, flooding into your conscious thoughts, and begin to steer you in all aspects of your life. Your ongoing journey into developing your intuition will therefore ensure that you can ask your dreams for help and they will reveal any answers you need.

Create a dream diary

Make it a habit to write down your dreams in a diary whether you do it jointly or alone. If you are working together on this chapter you can discuss your dreams if you wish. There are many different types of dreams, from the more mundane to the enlightened. The more in tune you are with each other, the more you will naturally filter into each other's dreams, as your souls will link up more readily in your sleep state. You can use this dream space to work on any problem-solving but we are going to focus specifically on using it to nurture your higher goals.

Even if you are working on this alone, your intent to use your intuition to focus positive energy on your relationship will influence your partner on a deeper level and your spirits will unite as soon as you both enter the dream state, although you may not remember their presence in any of your dreams.

To help ensure that you write down your dreams, use an attractive binder or notebook to remind you of this precious information. Get into the habit of writing down your dreams on a daily basis. And give each dream a number to help you keep track. You may wake up remembering one dream and drift off again on an entirely different mind adventure. Write down as much information as you can, immediately you wake, on scrap paper and then write it up in your diary when you have filled in any gaps. Flashes of information may come back to you through the day. When they do, make sure you add them to your diary while they are still fresh in your mind, but also remember to leave space for any insights and inspiration you may have on your dream when you read it back.

It's important to note the atmosphere of a dream and your feelings about it. It could be a bright sunny day, but you might feel lethargic, or alert. Write down whatever comes up in your dream, however odd it seems. Even if you don't understand, you may get a moment of clarity later on and suddenly have insight into its meaning. The more you use your intuition and the more you listen to your dreams, the clearer the guidance about your higher goal will become. You may wake up in the morning with a revelation about what you both need to learn spiritually; it may be about discovering more patience, compassion or having a flash of inspiration to take up a new creative skill that will encourage the boundless wise part of you to blossom. Then your mutual higher selves will work together to establish a stronger psychic link that will also help you overcome any obstacle in your path.

Here's how to set up a dream diary using one of my own as an example of a dream that imparts higher knowledge.

Example for setting up a psychic dream diary

Date: *14 January 2003*

Dream: *1*

Time: *Some time before 8 a.m.*

The dream: *I dreamed I gave birth to a baby called Sophia. I had an idea that the birth would be difficult, but it was remarkably easy, over in no time, with no pain. This pain-free birth struck me as different. The baby proved to be almost angelic. She was beautiful and healthy and didn't cry or cause me any distress or demand attention. I fed and nurtured her when I felt it was the right time, and she slept and gurgled and thrived without any concerns.*

Atmosphere: *Reassuring, uplifting, angelic goodness.*

Mood: *Learning to believe that things can be easy. I was surprised that everything was turning out so well.*

Signs and symbols: *An easy birth, an angelic baby girl, a house, me nurturing her, the name 'Sophia' which kept resounding throughout the dream as if there was a need for me to remember.*

Any associations: *Thinking about the publication of a document and how my ideas would be received. The name Sophia was so strong it stayed with me all the next day. I also had a hunch to look on the Internet and found a site dedicated to the name Sophia. Apparently Sophia signifies the mother and means wisdom. The site declared that the function of wisdom was to conceive. Babies also symbolise our creative potential. The dream was telling me that I had nothing to fear as I had given birth to a wise creation that would flourish without extra help. All I had to do was believe in its beauty.*

Connecting with your mutual goals

Think about your aspirations for several nights and before you go to sleep focus on what your joint higher goal is together. Writing down your aims on a piece of paper will help you to clarify your thoughts. If you are working on this together ensure that you both agree on what goals you want to pursue and both put the note under your pillows.

Allow yourself to relax and breathe deeply, then in your mind's eye imagine being given a catalogue with different topics listed in alphabetical order. By working on any of these subjects you can connect more to your specific goal. It could be about the different facets of love, intuition, healing or imparting knowledge or many other such subjects that could help you understand yourself better. If you want to know more about the different aspects of love, visualise flicking through the pages until you come to the letter L and see the different classes listed there. Look at the time your class is held during the night. A description might read:

L

Love: a facet of your spiritual goal
Techniques for opening the heart and learning about compassion, sympathy, support, trust and forgiveness. This will help you discover how important giving and receiving love is and that by using it you will heighten your consciousness and become closer to your spiritual goal.

This will provide a focal point for your mind and programme your dreams to lead you to the answers. Then imagine an angelic figure standing before you who will guide you to your class. To learn about this subject simply feel your desire to be in this class and remind yourself before you go to sleep, 'My class is at 3.30 a.m.' and trust that you will be there. In the morning write down the information that you dreamed about. Do bear in mind that you may not have an immediate conscious recollection, but you may have flashes of insight or more understanding of that subject than previously. The more you work towards this together, the more beneficial this will be as you will appear in each other's dreams and mutually explore your goals.

Take time to explore the different qualities and aspirations you want to learn about. You may not discover your goals immediately, but when you pick the right quality or subject you will suddenly feel a sense of recognition. Your goal is not a complicated test that you need to complete, but simply the quality that you need to expand and work with in order to be fulfilled on a soul level. This could be healing, which might mean learning a particular therapy or even taking time to nurture people within your family. Equally, it could be about teaching others to understand themselves better in whatever capacity that might be, whether as a teacher, counsellor, psychotherapist or lecturer. Perhaps you might use that skill within your own circle of friends. No one can tell you your goal; it is something that will feel right for you and it is one that you and your partner share, so clarify your feelings to each other if you are together. If not, continue to explore your dreams and intuition and you will soon discover your true spiritual destiny.

Now you have discovered how to use your dreams effectively to connect with your goals, know that you can also use them to heal any problems between you or help find ways of overcoming obstacles that present themselves in your life. Remember, your partner, more so than any other connection, is a powerful mirror for your mind energy. And this has been an opportunity to resolve the weaknesses within you by seeing them reflected back while you magnify your strengths.

Moving forward with your relationship

Let's take stock of what you have learned so far. You have focused your mind and used your imagination, creativity and dreams to strengthen the connection with your psychic self. In turn you have worked real magic on your relationship as you have healed and strengthened your soul mate bond and accessed powerful energy to build up the foundations of a strong and loving union. I hope you are inspired because the rewards are endless. By persistently using your finer qualities you will experience a deeper empathy, insight and unconditional love within your partnership and you will both feel more spiritually fulfilled as you recognise and work towards your joint spiritual goal. And the influence of your thoughts will generate a knock-on effect that will filter through to children, friends and family as they are affected by your positive, loving energy.

But don't feel that you need to stop now. You will find that many of the exercises in the past life chapter will benefit you, as many soul mate partnerships also connect through past lives they've shared. The questionnaire may have already revealed this, but take time to look through the rest of the book and see if any other exercises intuitively jump out at you. If they do, then your sixth sense is leading you to another way of developing your partnership.

Remember to finish with the last chapter to summarise what you have learned. You will probably be very surprised at the difference you will see in your growth when you have worked your way through the rest of the exercises.

Become addicted to your own potential; your soul mate energy will send you soaring to new heights as you embrace the spiritual destiny you were born to experience together.

THE PAST LIFE CONNECTION

A RELATIONSHIP WITH ITS ROOTS IN OUR ANCIENT HISTORY

He who has done his best for his time has lived for all times.

JOHANN VON SCHILLER, 1759–1805, GERMAN DRAMATIST, POET AND HISTORIAN

Those of you who have discovered that you have a past life link can now focus on the indelible attraction of this mysterious bond. This is the fascinating and at times bewildering connection you make when you meet someone you have known from a previous life. The attraction creates an undeniable recognition in both lovers as the historic energy that exists between you awakens an ancient memory and draws you together out of a mutual need for resolution. It may come as a surprise to know that this bond is remarkably common, as we all meet many people during the course of our lives with whom we have crossed paths and swords in a previous existence.

Here you can focus on the joy, frustration, challenges and thrill of this complex attraction. Although I am using expressions that sound contradictory, that is exactly what a past life attraction can be simply because of the many types of experiences we have gone through with one person. We not only have the gamut of emotional baggage from this lifetime but a whole host of other feelings, good and bad, which can be triggered when we are reunited with a centuries-old love.

This chapter will help you understand your past life attraction and tap in to the natural psychic empathy that you share through concentrating the powers of your higher mind. You now have the opportunity to evoke shared memories and heal any unresolved issues that arise between you.

It contains unique exercises designed for the nature of your bond where you will employ the four techniques of awareness so that you can focus your mind and bring your imaginative vision and dreams into play. By having trust and confidence in the exercises you can heal and strengthen your relationship. By identifying and understanding the many facets of emotions you have shared you can experience the pleasure of an enduring love to create a rock-solid foundation that will beneficially influence this lifetime and many future ones.

What is a Past Life Link?

A past life connection is when you meet someone with whom you have once shared a relationship in a previous incarnation. There is almost always an immediate attraction which can feel like a jolt of recognition or an intense magnetic pull which can evoke mixed feelings. For some people memories are quickly evoked in flashes of thoughts and dreams which reveal the threads of a shared past.

The way in which you react to each other can be bewildering at times. This is because your spirit and higher mind are eternal and it is this deeper essence that recognises the other person, whereas our personalities don't carry over from one lifetime to another and are unique to your current existence. As a result you can feel an overwhelming love and recognition towards someone, yet not understand their personality or relate to it. Remember, we all have auras (chapter two, page 20) which contain all the information about us, past and present. When we spiritually remember someone we are connecting with them on an energy level and it is a knowing without reason. Be prepared; sometimes a person may not be as consciously aware or even feel frightened of the deeper remembrance that is being evoked and find it hard to understand, particularly if they cannot accept that they are eternal selves who have lived many existences before this one.

In previous lives your current love may have been your mother, father, child, lover, or even your worst enemy. While it may seem almost incestuous when described in this way, from the higher perspective of our souls it is simply the thread of our spirits weaving through history in order to learn our spiritual lessons. It is through the divine law of karma (see below) that we all explore the many facets of human nature, experiencing different aspects of life in order to understand and learn more about who we are.

Our mind energy is eternal and just as we have weaknesses and strengths in this lifetime that we have to work with, we also have the residue of old emotions that can be triggered by this potent reunion of minds. A past life link reminds us that whatever legacy we have left behind us, we have yet another opportunity to heal, forgive and learn to love. Before you discover how your past life link affects your relationships, let's look at the subject of karma and the influence this powerful principle of cause and effect has on our lives.

Understanding Karma: the law of cause and effect

The Akashic records are known as the book of life, existing within the collective unconscious, which contains the entire history of every soul since the beginning of time. The records are impressed on a subtle substance called akasha, otherwise known as soniferous ether. That means that every thought, word, memory and action are recorded eternally in the universal filing system and can never be erased or forgotten. So none of us can avoid the effects of our thoughts and actions. Let's face it, a decision to behave in a certain way can affect not only our own lives but influence many others for better or worse.

This is where the wheel of karma comes into the equation. Many of us have heard the old expressions 'An eye for an eye and a tooth for a tooth' or 'What goes around comes around'. These adages concern this natural cycle of cause and effect. Karma is the divine law devised for the evolution of our souls so that we become conscious of the effects of what we do, think and say; no one can escape its influence.

We can recognise the effects of karma coming into play when there are certain people, challenges and circumstances that we find ourselves unable to walk away from, particularly within the intricate and at times complicated ties of our family. Relationships with our relatives often require some seriously difficult homework as we are faced with having to resolve problems or deal with a relatives' self-hate, mental illness or depression.

A learning experience

However, if you can think of your time on this planet as attending the earth school, then you will appreciate the law of karma keeping us aware of a crucial fact: that we have a responsibility for all our thoughts, feelings and actions not only towards others but also towards ourselves. All our trials, tribulations, sickness, mental illness and depression are merely a reflection of vengeful and aggressive actions that have been perpetuated by us in the past, and unexpressed and unresolved issues from not only our recent past but also our previous lifetimes. Instead of bewailing our fate, we have an opportunity to see our experiences and negative emotions with clarity as lessons to be learned. Remember that we attract facets of what we are in our connections to others. By becoming conscious of the way we react to people and developing our higher intuitive mind to connect us with our finer qualities of wisdom, love and understanding, we learn about the effects of our behaviour and how to begin to create good karma.

Individuals who are part of our learning cycle will often reincarnate to act out their roles with us again and again. Therefore someone to whom you have been drawn by an intensely strong magnetic attraction may have been connected to you in many incarnations. We share facets of mind energy with these people and that is why we are drawn into many experiences to play our parts as we mirror our lessons to each other.

But do note that karma is not an unfair judge and jury on all our sins, but simply a metaphysical dynamic carrying out the laws of the universe and dictating ultimate accountability for all that we create.

Don't forget the good karma

Remember, karma is not always bad! We have created good karma from our behaviour in past lives and we reap the benefits of karma in our current lives in our attitude towards others and ourselves. You see the signs of positive karmic patterns working when we are born with an already developed conscience, unique gifts and creative talents, ability to overcome adversity, positive thinking, wisdom, sound judgement and the fulfilment of a rewarding life that blossoms and flows. Benevolent good fortune is accrued from past and present lifetimes by nourishing the finer aspects of your own nature and aspiring to many qualities, such as discipline, maturity, self-responsibility, hard work, endurance, compassion, working on your spiritual growth, selflessness, overcoming obstacles, the development of your creative abilities, conscious behaviour, self-love and inner faith. Every effort in our past and present lives to further our own higher evolution is rewarded. And nothing ever goes unnoticed. It therefore makes sense to start taking responsibility for how we behave and think right now *by connecting and developing your higher intuitive faculties. Not only will you reap the benefits but your relationships will blossom and grow as a result.*

In his book Wisdom of the Mystic Masters *author Joseph J. Reed wrote the following expressions of cause and effect in the workings of karmic law. His thought-provoking comments may lend more insight into how we react to our circumstances.*

- *Aspirations and desires become abilities.*
- *Repeated thoughts become tendencies.*
- *Will to performance becomes action.*
- *Painful experiences become conscience.*
- *Repeated experiences lead to wisdom.*

Your past Life Lover

If you have discovered that you have a past life link then you will know what I mean by a sense of recognition or sense of feeling fated when you met your partner. You and your partner may fall into one of three distinct categories in the legacy of ancient reunions.

- You may have a soul mate bond with whom you have also experienced previous lifetimes. If so you will have an enduring unconditional love for each other regardless of any challenges you have had or are facing together. And you will aspire towards a joint spiritual destiny (see chapter four, page 119).
- You may have had many loving, constructive lives together and bond to experience certain lessons or challenges as a couple. For example, it may be that you don't have a karmic issue to overcome but that your partner is a catalyst for you to develop your courage, strength and patience. Or perhaps you need to recognise your own needs more and your lesson is simply to empower yourself and not be influenced by others.
- The third and most common category is when you are drawn together from a deeper mutual recognition to resolve past karmic problems that have occurred between you. You may recognise that distinct feeling towards someone as 'unfinished business', a sure sign that a liaison needs karmic rectification.

This last category leads to a more complex encounter as there is a strong magnetic attraction which in some cases can turn into a destructive compulsion to be near your lover at all times, or an addition to the energy feeling between you. This can occur particularly when an individual has many unresolved karmic issues that create feelings of insecurity and you or your partner may try to control and manipulate out of fear and instability. Don't kid yourself that this is a healthy, unconditional love. It most definitely is not.

It is important to understand, though, that these categories can still lead to misunderstandings and conflicts if you lose touch with your intuitive voice. But it is the 'unfinished business' side of past life relationships that can lead to complex relationships and if you are experiencing difficulties this may be a likely cause.

In order to understand irrational reactions in this context remember that destructive and negative behaviour in a present or previous incarnation to ourselves or others has left its mark on your unconscious mind. It remains unhealed until the behaviour is resolved and integrated within your subconscious. If we don't heal these old issues we repeat the same patterns of behaviour with a partner until we learn our lessons. This can be seen clearly when our worst fears are triggered in a relationship, whether a fear of abandonment, jealousy or irrational anger. You will know that this is true for you if you feel that you are going round in circles with your partner, never achieving a true meeting of minds.

That is why it is so important to use your inherent psychic gifts finally to heal the old karmic patterns and stop them recurring. To do this it is essential that you strive to be conscious of the way in which you think, feel and react that you began in chapter two. Only then can you release yourself from the old toxic emotion and experience the deep feeling of unconditional love and affinity that is rightfully yours.

To understand more about the complexities of the past life

connection, let's now focus on a couple who resolved the past karmic problems which were detrimentally affecting their relationship by learning to identify the reasons for irrational emotions.

Caroline's story: achieving happiness

'I first met David when I walked into the therapy centre where he worked as a nutritionist. I only went in for some advice but there was an instant feeling of recognition. David felt so familiar to me, it was like talking to an old friend and he obviously felt the same because five minutes later he'd invited me out for a drink.

'When we met three days later in a local pub, we talked all night long and from then on we were inseparable.

'The feeling that I had with David was completely different from anyone else I had ever met. I believed in the concept of re-incarnation but suddenly it was a reality and I knew with total certainty that we'd been together before. The feeling of "coming home" was uncanny.

'Then two months later I was left in no doubt. I started to have flashbacks to previous lives. It first happened when we were driving past a remote cottage in the Scottish Highlands near where we lived.

'I remember saying, "I've lived in a cottage like that before." I had a strong sense it had been Norway and in my mind I began to see fragmented pictures. It was like flicking through an old photo album very quickly. I was driving the car and pulled over to the side of the road and began relaying my memories to David about seeing lush green grass, geese and a white cottage. I had a strong sense of simply "knowing" it was around the tenth century. I was amazed when David said he'd had the same experience at the same moment. It confirmed to both of us that we were drawn together from an ancient shared past.

'A few weeks later I closed my eyes to relax when I was at home one afternoon. Once again, I saw pictures flashing through my mind. This time I was a priestess in a temple in Egypt and I saw myself wearing a white robe and gold jewellery on my arms. It appeared that David was an architect in that Egyptian period. I couldn't get any more information but I could sense that we knew each other very well.

'We were certainly blissfully happy together and within a year we had married. But suddenly out of the blue, David began to feel a deep paranoia about losing me. He would wake up in the middle of the night in a cold sweat, clutching my arm and saying, "You won't leave me will you?" I was concerned and reassured him, but then he got an irrational feeling of panic every time I went out without him. He would worry about my safety and keep phoning to check on me with a strained voice saying, "Are you okay. When will you get home?" We began talking about where these feelings of insecurity came from and whether I had done anything to provoke them. They were nothing to do with his childhood as he had a very secure upbringing. They seemed to be stemming from something more deep-rooted.

'One night when David felt frightened by the explosive emotions he was feeling and how it was affecting our relationship, I comforted him as we talked into the early hours. We were both determined to find a solution and our quest for answers seemed to have filtered into his dream state. David awoke in the middle of the night and told me how he had suddenly experienced a very real memory of a life with me in eighteenth-century southern France. We were both fruit farmers and married with eight children running around as we were busy with the day-to-day running of our orchard. He saw himself making furniture for our home, collecting apples and playing with our children. He experienced a feeling of total blissful happiness.

'Then he recalled me suffering from a fever that quickly took hold and all he could do was helplessly watch me die. He relived all the emotions of fear, anguish and loss. He never got over the loss and he could see that he had spent the rest of that lifetime grieving for me and this seemed to be the cause of his current paranoia.

'As he relayed the details of his dream I felt a familiar feeling that was ringing bells for me too and I was relieved that we had finally got to the bottom of the problem. The next day I waited for the signs of panic in his eyes when I went to leave the house, but thankfully he kissed me goodbye without batting an eyelid. He was once again at ease.

'We both believe that because he was able to identify the root cause of the problem, his fears completely disappeared from then on. We are once again contented and secure. We both know we have shared many lives together and other emotions may rise to the surface that could disrupt our marriage if we let them. We now see *how important it is not to repress negative or irrational feelings, but to identify, experience and release them. Only then can we keep our relationship open, honest and loving.'*

David and Caroline are a perfect example of a couple whose lives were disrupted by unresolved feelings from a past existence that were still festering in David's unconscious. By acknowledging there was a problem and trying to address it, they accessed their previous life history and were able to gain insight into why he felt as he did. These types of irrational fears can be activated suddenly and totally devastate your relationship if you do not take time to understand the knock-on effect of previous existences. Caroline chose not to judge her partner or blame herself for his reactions. They worked together to understand the cause, which enabled them to learn more about each other's past and move towards a positive outcome.

On an energy level, when feelings like this arise it is due to the second and fourth levels of the aura (emotions towards ourselves and others) being blocked (see chapter two, pages 30 and 38). Blockages occur when we suppress or don't deal with our negative emotions about ourselves or others and go into denial, over-obsess about them or turn to a prop such as food, alcohol or drugs to avoid them. If this happens our past life issues and old childhood traumas and beliefs will come back to haunt us, colouring the way we see things. It is then that we are imprisoned in our own torment akin to a living hell. We need to allow ourselves to experience our feelings in order to let them go. When we do release old feelings, we see ourselves and our partners more clearly. Our mind energy instantly expands and we become more connected with our inner voice, simply because we feel more integrated. Keep supporting each other to look deeper and focus on the eternal spirit within which was the core you in all your lives. This is where the voice of your sixth sense stems from. Then you can surmount any challenge or character faults that arise in your relationship and build a strong bond of invincible love that will serve you not only in this life but in many more to come.

Your Past Link Potential

The potential that you have with your partner is profound. When your relationship is working well you have a deep bond and an extraordinary empathy, as you have many experiences to draw on that help you explore the different sides of each other. You truly can be everything to each other and go beyond playing out the roles that society expects. You may have experienced glimpses of this already but when you are free of karmic issues that cloud your connection you can begin to explore each other's minds.

Negative karmic issues are our thought patterns of resentment and betrayal, vengeful feelings, guilt and misery that we carry from this life and the past. All these old feelings create blocks of frozen energy that show in our auric field and repress our vitality and zest for life. These blocks create barriers within us that make it hard to experience real intimacy. It means that we can overreact to simple situations or get a rush of anger, as we are unbalanced and therefore feel insecure. Much unconscious energy is required to hold on to these toxic emotions as any past trauma or negative feelings will freeze in time until they are healed. But as you bring issues to the surface by reconnecting with the past emotion and experiencing it, you also release masses of dammed-up energy that has been repressed through negative emotion.

You will feel the impact as energy starts flowing back into your body. You may get a tingling sensation in various parts of your body or feel lighter, happier and more at peace.

Consequently the resolution of old karmic issues has a huge effect on your psychic energy. Your mind energy will expand and you will experience a revitalised telepathic flow with your partner that brings you into a closer intimacy with more freedom of expression. Instead of being reactive you are understanding and empathetic. If you focus on the eternal spirit in both of you, you can look behind the personality to what is really going on. At your very best you can guide each other with the experience of all your previous history, understanding each other's gifts and flaws and remaining supportive. You are there to help each other understand how to heal the pain of the past and experience your love as timeless and unconditional.

Now we will look at any detrimental aspects of your relationship that the questionnaire in chapter three has highlighted that are undermining your partnership. If you answered yes to more than one of the questions in the destructive section this has revealed some negative elements in your relationship that need to be healed. Here is your opportunity to take the steps to move forward constructively.

Destructive Tendencies

If you discovered that the questionnaire revealed destructive tendencies in your relationship, this chapter will help you to focus on using your psychic powers to bring out the hidden potential in your relationship. Your response to those specific questions revealed unresolved issues and destructive tendencies that are adversely affecting your relationship.

Review the way you react towards your partner. Couples with a past life link often habitually push each other's button when there are problems that are not being resolved. If you are feeling jealous, angry, uneasy and are living in a state of conflict or constant arguments then this behaviour is evidence in itself. It is important to become aware of what you are triggering in each other and why. Don't persuade yourself that you are living passionately or experiencing deep love when you are on an exhausting rollercoaster of arguments and reconciliations.

It may be that you have allowed yourself to be boxed into playing a role that stops you developing yourself and your partnership. Perhaps you are the dominant one in the relationship, always getting your own way while your partner lets you carry on, continuing a pattern of past life behaviour. But you are not learning any lessons by doing this. Equally, maybe you have taken the passive role and won't confront your loved one because you prefer an easy life. Do you always act like a needy child, not wanting to take responsibility? Or the responsible adult taking care of everything in your lives? If you recognise that you are acting out a role, then you need to step out of the mould that you have allowed yourself to fit into.

Whatever your situation or however bad things have become, know that you can find a better way of relating to each other which is more loving, compassionate, wiser and honest than ever before. All you have to do is focus with your deeper intuitive knowledge on the finer qualities that you both share.

We are all multi-faceted individuals with many ways of relating to others. The more you can be yourself, the more of an adventure your partnership becomes as you can be all things to your partner.

Understanding love and power

Power issues can occur with a current partner when you have past life links. This happens because of the many dimensions of emotional dynamics that we go through playing out our myriad roles in order to learn who we are. To see how much you have evolved in your understanding of love and power simply ask yourself the question, 'What is love and what is power?' There is no judgement on your answer; your response is simply a reflection of your own consciousness. So answer this question now and then again at the end of the book. Periodically throughout your life write down your response to this question. Then look back at your answers months, years and decades later. I promise you will be amazed as you see your own evolving growth recorded in front of you.

Feelings of Disconnection

If the questionnaire revealed feelings of disconnection between you at times, this is because you have allowed unresolved issues to come between you and create a barrier. If you have stopped relating to each other honestly or shelved problems at the back of your mind instead of finding solutions, then your relationship with your partner will become more distant. The reason for this goes back to my comments in chapter two about all thoughts being fuelled by emotion, which is stored in our auras (see page 17). It is normal for every person to have a residue of emotion and stress from everyday life that needs to be released. The longer negative feelings are stored the more they will make you feel irritable and depressed as you not only block the way you feel about yourself but you suppress other more positive emotions from rising to the surface. By not communicating your thoughts and emotions honestly you stop yourself from loving your partner and yourself. This creates a barrier that will make you feel bored and in a rut. How can a relationship be loving, passionate and exciting when you do not feel that you can speak openly and be spontaneous?

It is easy to fall into this state after a long time together or in order to avoid conflict and live an apparently easier life. But the price you pay is huge when you become so distant from each other that you feel more like disconnected strangers. When I say respond honestly, though, I mean doing so with tact and diplomacy, not just blurting out things without any concern for your partner's feelings. Otherwise your honesty, which has the potential to heal, can create even more conflicts between you.

If you have more than three yes answers regarding your feelings of disconnection, it may be that you have both detached from each other to the extent that you cannot connect properly. You've allowed too much emotion and pain to become buried inside you. You need to find your way back once again to how you both feel about who you are and your relationship. You have an opportunity to give your partnership the kiss of life that it so desperately needs and have faith that the exercises will reconnect you to each other. It may feel initially scary to allow yourself to get in touch with your deeper feelings but it is for the sake of your future happiness that you do so.

However, don't live your life doing what you feel you ought to do instead of what you want to do. If you cannot be honest with your partner, at least be honest with yourself and move on from a relationship that cannot work. Let's look at why it's so important for you to make that choice, and act on it.

Knowing when it's time to move on.

It's time to walk away from your relationship if you feel uncomfortable about getting close to your partner or if ongoing conflicts have become a way of life. You will already know clearly whether your partnership has become too destructive to be fixed or that feelings have been repressed for too long for you to turn things around. You have to have trust, vision and a desire to make things work when you focus on the psychic exercises in this book. Destructive past life relationships can often result in power struggles where one of you always has to back down. You both have to want to make the effort, accept each other's point of view and want the same things. And you must accept that it takes humility, knowing that you have got things wrong, and a willingness to try another way – the way of your higher intuitive mind. If you feel that you want to make things work, but your partner is only interested in getting their own needs met or doing things their way, or vice versa, then neither of you will have the joint vision required to create a deeper loving bond.

When our intuitive self takes the lead there are no power struggles, control issues or demands. We act with compassion, love, understanding and trust. But when our ego and insecurities make the decisions, in extreme cases we become control freaks who want everything our own way or doormats, relinquishing our responsibility for ourselves and our relationships. Unfortunately, some people are so entrenched in karmic issues within themselves they cannot step out of the mental and emotional pattern they have created to rise above to a clearer view. It may be that you or your partner has spent many lifetimes expressing this type of behaviour. If so then they may be unable to see themselves with any lucidity or insight and therefore cannot change. People like this believe they are always right and cannot go through life without creating conflicts or obstacles. Relationships with these people quickly become unhealthy and can ruin your life. This will inevitably hold you back from developing yourself emotionally and intuitively and will block you from finding the love and growth that you can enjoy with someone new. Only you can know whether your relationship can be salvaged or not. Trust in your higher mind by continuing to develop your intuition and use the exercises in this book, and you will soon discover the right pathway for you; have the courage and faith to act on your decision.

Understanding and Healing Your Past Life Connection

Once you have looked at your relationship with honesty, you need to decide whether you are committed to strengthening it and reconnecting to that ancient bond between you. If you are, then you will discover that whatever the conflicts you are experiencing, whether based on disinterest, disillusionment, anger or fear, they can be resolved as you stimulate your intuitive powers as mentioned in chapter three, page 62. This higher frequency of energy is induced when you learn to respond from your inner voice and develop your psychic powers; this means you now have an incredible opportunity to learn how to love from the highest part of yourselves.

Developing your psychic awareness enables you to enter into a higher state of consciousness where you can access the Akashic record of past experiences, including a previous existence, through your dreams, intuition, visualisation, self-hypnosis, hypnotherapy or meditation. The rest of this chapter will help you to understand further the past life connection and will give you powerful ways in which you can use your psychic powers to create a more honest, passionate and expressive connection with your partner to appreciate and explore all the facets of the selves you have been and can enjoy together.

We now come to the first of the specially formulated exercises that will engage the intuitive powers of your mind. These exercises employ the second and third techniques of focusing your mind and using your imagination in myriad ways to channel and develop your psychic powers. Each exercise is an evolving process: the initial one enables you to clear out old negative issues and awaken a deeper psychic connection with yourself. The next one will enable both you and your partner to connect with any issues from previous lives and bring them to the surface to be healed so that you can begin to reconnect on a deeper level. From then on each exercise will be geared for you to focus your intuitive powers on your partner to rekindle the spark between you and awaken unconditional love. The higher mind is stimulated when it is surprised and the different ways in which you approach the exercises will prompt your psychic awareness to grow as well as develop your partnership bond on a deep, intuitive level.

Those with a genuine past life connection often experience a strong psychic bond in the same way that soul mates do and have a telepathic link with their partners. This can be because many soul mates have also shared past lives. But even if you are not soul mates the ongoing connection you have experienced through many incarnations has created an emotional resonance. It is precisely because you have experienced past lifetimes together that unresolved issues from the past may arise within your partnership and block your intuition. You may have been drawn together with a mutual mission in mind. Perhaps it is one of unfinished business to help you release yourself from any residual past pain. That is why it is so important to activate and strengthen your intuition so that you create a positive outcome and do not perpetuate old problems through being blinkered. Equally, consider that your partner is a catalyst for your growth and that you are learning to develop certain qualities in your character that you previously lacked such as resilience, compassion and understanding.

The following exercise is an essential launch pad into your psychic awareness as it will expand your higher mind and bring old issues from your previous lives to the surface, enabling you to clear out emotional blocks that you have repressed. This is crucial to clear your aura of any issues that may consciously or unconsciously be causing friction and barriers between you. Once you have freed yourself from some of this baggage and connected with other aspects of yourself, your intuitive energy, previously dammed up, will flow more freely. You will have laid the foundations so that you are ready to move on to the next exercise with a clear mind and an open heart. In this relaxed state you will be ready to reconnect and build a deeper bond with your partner.

Heal the emotions of your past

Lie down and breathe deeply several times. Feel yourself sinking into yourself, until you are aware of nothing but your own mind. Detach yourself from any thoughts and simply witness your own thinking process.

Now visualise high in the sky, far above the clouds, a colossal temple, more regal and imposing than anything you have ever seen. As you look at it you can see its huge ornate double doors with polished marble steps leading up to the entrance. Focus on bringing this stunning piece of architecture into your mind in as much detail as possible. The doors are placed under huge arches and there are minute gemstones of every description embedded into the walls of the temple, which sparkle in the light. See yourself walking up the stairs towards the doors. Feel the marble beneath your feet as you ascend each step. As you approach the doors they miraculously swing open to reveal an unbelievably high ceiling which seems to reach almost one hundred feet. Take a deep breath and then step inside. There is an immediate sense of peace and tranquillity within this colossal sanctum and you are immediately affected by the all-pervading stillness. There is a strong sense of divine energy and you feel awed as well as deeply relaxed and calm. It's as if you have entered a timeless place.

As you look around the immense, opulent room filled with thousands of different-sized candles positioned on the walls, you see ten-foot-high paintings by many past masters such as Rubens and Botticelli spaced along the walls. There are magnificent stained-glass windows with varied hues of every colour, and shafts of light fall across the shining marble floor, creating rainbow effects. As you walk through the room you notice that your footsteps echo around the building and in the distance you can hear the resonant tones of a clear temple bell. At the back of the room you see crystal shelves covered with precious stones of all shapes and colours from emeralds, sapphires, diamonds to pieces of amber, jade and resin. There is a sense of beauty and wisdom emanating from the very walls of this sacred building. You can discern a light scent of incense and once again you are entranced by the powerful calming atmosphere that is steeped in history.

Look along the marble walls for a door. It is not easy to pick out, but feel your hands slide along the marble and eventually you will see a small gold door handle. When you open it, you see some old stone steps that lead down towards the cellars. You feel an urge to explore and as you proceed down each step, feel the well-worn stone beneath your feet as you descend deeper and deeper into the depths of the building.

At the foot of the steps an elderly man awaits you. He looks at you expectantly with large, kind eyes that peer over gold spectacles and his face is almost swamped by his long white hair and beard. He is wearing a long dark gown that reaches the floor and you know instantly that he is the guardian of all the records of your past lives.

When he asks why you are here explain your quest for self-knowledge and to heal and understand the nature of your current relationship, naming your partner. The old man listens attentively, then bows his head and grants your request.

He beckons you to follow him into the historic library. You seem to glide behind the flapping coat tails of his gown as he leads you through a labyrinth of endless corridors past shelf after shelf piled high with books. Eventually he stops at a shelf of stacked volumes of all sizes. He pauses for a few moments as he assesses them and you can see that your name is inscribed on the shelf in gold embossed lettering. Verify to him that this is indeed the name by which you are known in this lifetime, then survey the books on the shelf. There are many of them, some thin, some thick, all representing each of your past lives and the experiences between your lives. Observe the chronological order of your life and, as the guardian looks at you questioningly, reiterate that it is the most relevant past life in relation to healing your current relationship that you wish to understand.

Now when you cast your eyes back over the shelf all the books will appear faint except for the one most pertinent to your request, which will immediately stand out. The guardian immediately reaches for this thickly bound record and hands it to you. Feel the weight of this volume and the texture of the soft leather cover and know that when you open the pages you will observe the shared experiences between you and your present partner. When you open this you have no fear of what you might find. What you will see has already happened and presents no surprise to your subconscious. You are merely looking at the record of your experience. As you flick through the pages you notice there are also snapshots of memories once shared and an audio tape that may automatically play when you come to certain pages.

You feel drawn to a chapter in the book that is relevant to you now; absorb the information serenely and allow it to seep into your mind. You have all the time you want. You may see snapshots of past memories flashing through your mind, feel sudden emotions or have a sense of knowing about the past. Whatever you see or feel, don't judge yourself, even if you get nothing. Trust and have confidence that you are experiencing just what you need to. When it feels right hand the volume back to the guardian who is waiting patiently some distance away. He replaces the record on the shelf and beckons you to follow him once again as he leads you through the maze of corridors to the old stairway back to the temple.

When you arrive at the staircase you thank him and bid him farewell, ascend the stairs and proceed through the small door to arrive back in the serene majesty of the temple. Take a deep breath, slowly exhale and then pause for a while as you survey the beauty of this divine place. Silently thank this celestial sanctum for helping to guide you to a place of healing and resolution. The doors once again open automatically and you descend the huge stone steps. As you place one foot in front of the other, you feel your consciousness returning to you and by the time you reach the foot of the stairs you feel more aware. Sense yourself back in your room in your house and review your experience.

This experience is cleansing and liberating. By consciously bringing forth buried memories of previous lives pertinent to your current circumstances you are freeing yourself and your partner from the repressed or unresolved issues that are blocking you from expressing your intuitive self. When you express your psychic self and that higher part of you takes the lead, then you purge these inner issues and you no longer need to experience ongoing conflict and misery within your relationship.

Questions to ask yourself

1. If you are wondering how long it takes for information to filter through, take note that some people find they immediately become aware of memories from a past life. Some of you may have to repeat this visualisation several times until information seeps through to your conscious minds. Those of you who are natural visualisers and have begun developing your intuition or who are already very creative (see chapter three) will find your efforts

rewarded with a stream of images or a sense of knowing. Other insights may be revealed in your dreams but keep a notebook to hand in case any intuitive flashes come through during your everyday life.

2. If you find that you haven't received any information it may be that you are encountering resistance to your previous experiences which is blocking the knowledge from coming through. If so, it may be that you are fearful about what you might see and perhaps you are not ready subconsciously to receive and heal this information. If so, keep developing your psychic powers and continue with this visualisation and other exercises in this chapter: eventually the floodgates will open.

Further development

If you are working on this with your partner you can discuss what came up for you and you can both consciously work on your relationship together. But if not, keep on with the visualisation and know that you are well on the way to overcoming any barriers; you can go back into this temple at any time and access other past lives that can help you.

If you don't have problems in your relationship this exercise will enable you to understand yourself and each other and bond more deeply. This visualisation is also a way of strengthening and expanding your higher mind via your imagination. As a consequence, you will automatically feel lighter and more intuitive as you release old emotions and find that you are better able to empathise with your partner on a deeper level. As your responses towards your partner change, they too will start to relate to you in a more loving way.

You have built a bridge with your intuitive eternal self and begun to bring old thoughts and emotions to the surface to be healed. Even if you haven't yet seen anything tangible, the process has already begun on an unconscious level. You may feel exhausted and need to sleep so that your dream state can help clarify things. Or you may feel angry, weepy or fearful. Equally, you may feel elated as the energy released sends a revitalised surge of energy through you. Whatever you feel, keep allowing yourself to experience the emotions and simply say 'thank you' in your mind. Saying thank you means that you allow yourself to experience this feeling and accept the emotion as a lesson to be understood, so that you can then integrate it within your mind. Whatever you feel is unique to you but from now on keep clearing away any emotions that rise to the surface.

You have taken an important first step in cleansing and strengthening your bond. But allowing emotions to come to the surface and releasing them must continue if you want your relationship to blossom and grow constructively. Otherwise you will always be a slave to your old thought patterns.

To illustrate how this might happen, read about a woman whose unresolved issues from a past life constantly affected the way she reacted in relationships and how they finally destroyed the one partnership that really needed to be healed, by letting her festering emotions get the better of her.

Katie's story: the break-up

Katie was a thirty-year-old woman with a relationship history that read like a shopping list. She had experienced many short-lived relationships that always ended disastrously. And the problems were always the same: her tendency to become clingy and paranoid with all her boyfriends, thinking that they were going to leave her. The emotional hysterics were in contrast to her image as a fiercely independent and dynamic sales executive. As a petite brunette she was always vivacious and assertive and she herself couldn't understand her own irrational behaviour.

Her last failed partnership lasted just eight months and had filled her with despair. John was a partner in the business she worked in and was loving, considerate and reliable. But within weeks of being with him, the old patterns of her behaviour emerged – only this time her irrational behaviour was amplified. She was suspicious of anyone who telephoned him, thinking it was another woman, and she began asking him questions about other women whom she thought he might find attractive. Even an innocent comment about an actress on television would make her panic and wonder if he'd gone off her. Poor John liked her so much that he constantly reassured her, saying 'I wouldn't be with you if I didn't want you.' But nothing would make her feel secure. She was convinced that he would eventually leave her for someone else who was prettier and more successful.

She had no reason not to trust him, as he showered her with affection and they spent nearly every night together. But one afternoon she saw him hugging an attractive woman outside the office at lunchtime. Her paranoia got the better of her and she ran up to him in a state of hysteria and started hitting him in front of the woman, screaming, 'I knew I couldn't trust you.' Eventually the man grabbed both her hands and the woman he'd been talking to called the police on her mobile, saying, 'Please come quickly, my brother's being attacked.' When Katie heard those words she stopped in her tracks and looked at the woman sheepishly and then slowly turned to look at John. His voice was echoing in her ears as she heard him say softly, 'Yes, Katie, you heard that right, this is my sister Eleanor.' Katie was beside herself with embarrassment as she could see the derisory look in his sister's eyes and she sloped off back to her desk feeling pathetic. The police call was cancelled but John rang her that night to leave a message on her answerphone, saying, 'I'm sorry, Katie, but I can no longer handle this situation. Being with you is like being with a firework that could go off at any minute.'

Katie felt angry with herself and these seemingly uncontrollable behavioural patterns that had escalated in her relationship with John. She decided to seek help from a hypnotherapist to get to the bottom of why she reacted this way, never trusting or giving relationships a chance.

Within the first hour of her session she experienced many past lives where she had been a man. In one pertinent lifetime she saw herself as a man madly in love with a beautiful society woman. This woman was everything Katie as a man had wanted in that past lifetime: feminine, nurturing and alluring and she recognised this woman as her recent boyfriend John. They were due to marry, but suddenly she saw another episode of that lifetime where the woman was telling him that she was marrying someone else, a man who could offer her the status and wealth her family wanted for her. Experiencing the emotions of the man she had once been, Katie relived the devastation and sense of betrayal that she had experienced then. The revelation quickly dawned that she had never got over the shock and betrayal of losing the woman she had loved in her lifetime as a man.

Now she was flooded with the feelings of loss that the past memories had evoked. She realised afterwards how male she was in her attitudes in this lifetime, being very assertive and competitive at work. Her fears stemmed from not feeling good enough about who she was, and this destructive pattern was simply a repressed emotion from an old lifetime. As a man she had lost the love of someone she had adored to someone supposedly better. Until she allowed herself to become consciously aware of this buried feeling she couldn't bring it to the surface to be healed and it was blocking her ability to trust anyone intimately, particularly John. He had experienced a complete role reversal in their union, but she had to reconcile her feelings from their past liaison.

Katie's story has clarified how destructive, unresolved emotions from a past life can wreak havoc. Despite having a loving partner, her old thought patterns had created an irrational reaction, which left a trail of disaster. Katie didn't know any different and was a victim of her old emotional self. Fortunately, you have a choice. By using the higher psychic powers of your mind you no longer have to be a victim of karmic circumstances, allowing old thought patterns to annihilate your relationships. Whatever your personal circumstances, you can now practise an exercise that will create a stronger, more intimate bond, helping you to connect more deeply with each other and open the doors to unconditional love.

Strengthening your connection

Having done the groundwork in the previous exercise to bring unresolved issues to the surface, you will now be ready to work with your partner and allow issues from other lives that need to be healed to come to the surface. Once you allow these to surface into your conscious awareness these conflicts or negative feelings won't overshadow you both and influence your reactions to each other. You will then find it easy to connect on a deeper bond of loving energy that can flow between you unhindered by stress or misunderstandings.

In this next stage you will focus your mind by looking into your partner's eyes. This will enable your intuition to come to the fore and you will see the many faces of your partner's past lives. You will send loving waves of higher psychic energy towards your partner, which will allow you to connect on a core level with the deeper essence of your partner and to use your intuition to see beyond their persona to who they were. Your higher minds will open up and begin to link and the love that you send them will create a powerful feeling of unity and telepathy. This powerful dynamic will affect your relationship on an intrinsic level to create more trust, empathy, honesty and a profound intimacy.

You will obtain a more powerful result if you and your partner work together by sitting opposite each other, and take it in turns to do the exercise. But if you want to do the exercise alone or your partner does not want to participate then place a clear photograph of them in front of you.

Close the curtains so the room is dark, and light some candles. This atmosphere will help you to relax and your mind to focus in a different way and see things in the shadowy contours of each other's faces. Take a deep breath, relax and listen to some soothing background music if you wish. Become aware of your own energy field by sensing the energy around your body and head extending out from you by around three feet. Imagine you are touching the far side of the wall with your energy and sense what that feels like. Now feel as if you are touching the ceiling and note how it feels. This will help you to feel centred and more conscious of your own aura, which will help you to align with your intuitive self.

Study your partner's face and focus on their forehead so you are not looking directly into their eyes. Then drop your gaze and look deeply into their eyes and note their expression. Don't try to see anything, just relax. If your partner is sitting opposite they do not have to respond in any way other than to look back at you.

Some people get better results if they look into the eyes and others if they focus on the forehead area. Go with whatever works for you. Continue to look at them for around five minutes and during this time see if any other images are superimposed on their face that change their expression. Does their face suddenly change shape, or do they suddenly seem more male than female or vice versa? Can you see them dressed from another other time? Don't struggle to see this, just allow whatever happens to happen. Now close your eyes and ask in your own mind; 'What is the lifetime that is creating problems and holding us back? Reveal yourself as the person I once knew so that the cause of our unresolved issues can surface.' Open your eyes and focus on your partner or the photograph again and say this once more in your mind. Your intuition can help you to see who this person was before and their relevance to your current situation. Keep focusing and see if their face changes. It may be that instead of their face altering images flash through your mind or you hear something telepathically. Your psychic powers can work in many ways and concentrating on their face is a way of focusing the mind.

Now visualise loving, golden energy pouring from your heart chakra, in the centre of your chest and flooding into your partner, filling up their aura field with golden light. As before, you can visualise this happening whether your partner is physically in front of you or through the photograph. Feel your unconditional love as this light energy encompasses them and flows into their heart chakra. It is important to feel this energy coming from your heart and not the emotional centre of your solar plexus, as heart energy is unconditional, while solar plexus energy can be tied up with other emotional issues and expectations. As you visualise this energy you will feel a sense of uplift. And at the same time you are raising your own consciousness. By doing this you get a sense of perspective, as you see a bigger picture rather than focusing on any misunderstandings.

The effects of this exercise can be transformational. Focusing on your partner's face has a powerful effect in many ways. By looking into their eyes like this you are looking deep into their essence beyond all the layers of their past personas. You may see a glimpse of who they were rise to the surface and the love you send them will help to heal the cause of the emotion. Once you see a facet of who they once were coming through, their energy will affect you on a more profound level as you bring the issue to the surface. But also by looking deeply into your partner's eyes you are connecting on a deeper level of intimacy and recognising them for who they are beneath all the varied masks of personality.

Questions to ask yourself

1. Did you find it easy to see different faces superimposed over your partner's face? Or did you get a sense of former shared lives or issues? Perhaps you received flashes of information, which could come as a fast-moving slide show or telepathic thoughts. If you didn't get any of these things, don't worry. You are intuitive and you must trust that this information may come in different ways. Your psychic powers are inherent within you; you may need to relax more to tap in to them. If there is a wall between you and your partner that has resulted from tension, fear or a lack of trust, it may be difficult initially to get past this.

   Have faith that you have made a huge leap in the right direction by making this start. Whether you know it or not things have already changed on a subtle energy level simply because of your focused, healing mind energy being directed at them. You may find that you have a series of dreams over the next few nights that will give you more insight. Otherwise practise this exercise again at the end of the chapter and see if you glean more from it.

2. Did you find it easy to send love from your heart? This exercise is very cleansing and healing as you feel your love pouring into your partner. If it was hard to do, it may be that you have many defences between you. Keep practising feeling love coming from your heart and flowing towards them whenever you have a spare five minutes. The more you send this energy, the more your partner will respond lovingly.

This exercise will have enabled you to bring unresolved problems to the surface so that you can connect deeply with your partner and create more love and understanding between you. Even if your partner was not physically present and you were focusing on a photograph they will have unconsciously felt the impact of your powerful thought energy and love. Don't underestimate this; the powers of your mind will work and the pure energy that you sent from your heart will create more healing. Don't intellectualise what happens between you or over-examine it. Simply by allowing your feelings to flow, your intuitive powers will heighten and you will begin to awaken unconditional love. Remember, unconditional love has the same frequency as your intuitive powers (see page 8). The more you use both, the stronger they become.

The exercises you have undertaken are designed to enable you to expand your higher mind and develop your intuition. You should already have seen a marked transformation in your relationship. Connecting with your partner on an intuitive level and focusing on their essence means that you will feel a deeper intimacy and affinity. You will feel more in tune with each other, which will affect your responses to each other. Your newly charged auric field will vibrate to a more loving frequency as your focused intent in the exercises sends out healing vibrations. This will influence our body language and behaviour and you will naturally want to be more loving, compassionate and considerate towards your past life lover.

But there are changes happening on a deeper level that affect your partner more than just your attitude. In the past your partner may have ignored loving behaviour if they were stressed or irritable. Now they will not be able to help but respond positively to the unconscious waves of loving energy influencing their mind and emotions.

Here we turn to the lessons from a past life connection and how another mind-focusing tool can enable you to bond and empathise with your partner on a deep psychic level.

What we learn from a past life link

You have seen some of the ways in which an experience from a past life can affect relationships. These karmic lessons of jealousy, fear and betrayal are facets of the many emotions we can carry with us from one lifetime to another until they are healed. We can evolve and create good karma for ourselves with a past life partner if we connect with our intuition and higher minds; when we are in tune with our inner voice we have wisdom, empathy and understanding of how to respond to situations. However, sometimes you can feel like a victim of a past life relationship when you want to work on it and heal it but your partner would prefer to move on or stay stuck in the same old patterns.

If you are in this situation you must remember that underlying every karmic partnership, however challenging the circumstances, is the need to learn spiritual lessons from your past life lover. Whatever conflicts you are facing, behind the façade your partner is a mirror to help you see yourself more clearly. These lessons are repeated until you take on board what these issues are teaching you.

Often a learning curve continues through incarnations with the same characters taking part in our story, until a lesson is finally understood and we break the cycle. The next story about Margaret reveals the effects of her husband's adultery and how she discovered that her husband and his mistress were recurring players in her past life history. In this situation the choice of remaining in the relationship was taken out of her hands. But rather than assuming we are victims of fate when faced with betrayals in relationships, her experience shows how important it is to look beyond the surface attitudes of our partner's behaviour and to see the lesson behind the circumstances. Only then can we alter the recurring negative patterns of our past lives and heal ourselves so that we stop the misery of repeating the same experiences.

Margaret's story: the betrayal

Margaret was in her late forties when she discovered her successful husband Gerald was leaving her for another woman. She came home from shopping one day and found a scrawled message saying bluntly, 'I'm leaving.'

Margaret was in shock and could do nothing but collapse in a chair and sob uncontrollably. She couldn't understand why this had happened. She had been the dutiful corporate wife to her rich lawyer husband for over twenty years. With her three children now grown up, she thought she could look forward to a more enjoyable future. When she contacted her husband at work, he refused to meet her and told her tersely that he had met another woman who was his soul mate and would be filing for divorce.

She was devastated when she was told through the grapevine that the 'other woman' was in fact a well-known fashion designer. Margaret spent the next days with her head in a whirl. She had always suffered from low self-esteem, but over the next few nights a morbid fear set in and she became convinced that this new woman would steal her children away from her. At the time she couldn't understand the irrationality of her emotions, as her children were adults, the youngest being eighteen, yet she would tremble at the thought of it. Worse was to come as she soon discovered that her husband had cancelled all her credit cards and she was deeply concerned about how she would live day to day. She had never had a job and had always relied on housekeeping from her husband to buy what she needed.

She also didn't know how she was going to stand her ground in a divorce court, as her husband was a renowned lawyer with a ferocious temper, now with an equally powerful girlfriend. With such an uncertain future, in desperation she decided she needed help and went to see a hypnotherapist to improve her confidence levels.

Despite not intending to have a past life regression, information quickly came to the surface about the characters in her present drama. What unfolded opened her eyes to her husband's betrayal and his attraction to his present mistress.

As Margaret relaxed in the chair she suddenly saw herself as a farm hand who was working on the land of a wealthy landowner. As old memories resurfaced she saw that she was having an affair with the farmer and had got pregnant. But the farmer's wife discovered what was going on and the baby was taken away from her as soon as she had given birth, and the rich farming couple raised it as their own. She thought the farmer would take care of her financially but she never got a penny from him. Instead she was treated with contempt and was forced to continue working on the farm with the pain of seeing her child being reared by the couple. In that life she felt she had no choice but to keep quiet and accept the situation.

In this amazing past life scenario Margaret instantly recognised the farmer as her current husband, but also recognised that his wife in this past life was his current mistress. She realised why she had such an irrational fear that her grown-up children would be taken away, after being forced to hand over her newborn baby.

After this impromptu regression, Margaret gained confidence. She realised that she always played the same part and was now seen as the mousy corporate wife who wouldn't answer back. She had several more regressions in the following weeks that revealed her husband had often lived lives as the rich aggressor and his mistress had shared many lives with him as his wife. This explained their compelling attraction in this lifetime. She, however, was always on the sidelines left with nothing. This was the first life where she was his wife and not the bit on the side, but she had still not learned to stand up for herself, allowing him to perpetuate the role of tyrant.

As the divorce proceedings continued it was evident that her husband wanted to leave her with nothing, despite their many years together. This time Margaret knew she couldn't remain the victim of circumstance and had to stand up for her rights. Previously she had felt she was caught in a spider's web, but now she could see the pattern of a much larger picture.

Her courage grew so that she was able to stand up against him, asked for court extensions and got the divorce settlement she knew she was entitled to. This made up for her many lifetimes of being left with nothing. Her husband was aghast at the change in her character and phoned her one evening to shout, 'You're not the woman I knew!' Margaret felt a release of ancient victimhood as she stepped into her new role and replied confidently, 'No, now I'm a woman who believes she's worth something.' And on that note she forgave her husband, seeing the spiritual lesson he had taught her, bought a plane ticket and flew off to the Caribbean to enjoy the fruits of her well-earned labours. She now feels empowered and more content than ever before and relishes her new-found autonomy.

Margaret's story reveals a woman who had spent her current and previous lifetimes accepting a bitter fate as the eternal victim who could never recognise her own power and take control of her destiny. Yet on a higher level her husband had been a great catalyst for her to develop strength and courage. Someone like this may appear to be an enemy but on a soul level they could be your greatest friend and teacher as they provoke you to change your behaviour.

For anyone who has experienced a miserable relationship, look at the role you have played. Have you played the victim or allowed someone to dominate you? You may find, even in your current lifetime, that you are on the receiving end of a tyrant or bully. Bear in mind that this is a lesson you need to understand so that you can learn courage and autonomy. Equally, if you are always dominating your partner or being dishonest, you need to be conscious of the future consequences of your actions.

But the law of 'cause and effect' works in many ways and Margaret's story illuminates how karma isn't just about scoring points or being on the receiving end of what you dish out. Although it might seem that you have swallowed a very bitter pill in your own life, there is a higher karmic law in place that knows how we need to develop our characters and evolve for our own good.

Don't preoccupy yourself with what your partner needs to learn, as their issues aren't relevant to your life. Whatever real-life drama you play out, you are the principal player for your own soul. The actors taking part reappear not just in future lives but in your current life so that you can finally see how you can respond differently and change an ongoing cycle. So whatever roles you play, know that you can change the way you respond to circumstances. Whether you decide to remain with a past life lover or walk away you can discover how the inherent power of your intuition can connect you with unresolved past lives.

The next stage will amplify your psychic powers and work on strengthening your bond. This exercise is the next step in reigniting the spark between you as you harness a powerful empathetic link and allow your mind energy to merge with your loved one. The overall effect is to bring about a synergy that allows you to experience that profound sense of feeling at one with your partner.

Using intuitive empathy to bond with your partner

Having a past life connection means you have a strong emotional dynamic and as you bring any issues to the surface to be healed you will experience a powerful psychic synergy. It is only when you don't resolve problems that barriers arise between you and you enter into power struggles, irrational behaviour or depression. Creating empathy on a deeper level, particularly for past life lovers, is a crucial aspect to developing your intuitive higher self as it strengthens your higher mind and enables you to connect with the deeper aspects of who you are and rise above the limitations of past and present problems.

Once you use your empathic feelings regularly you can experience a greater feeling of intuitive bonding and fulfilment.

The following exercise will help you to use your higher mind more and heighten your empathic awareness. This is particularly pertinent for past life lovers as you explore more of who your partner is now. And who they are now is a culmination of the many selves that they have been before, strengths that they have earned and weaknesses that they are striving to work on. To do this you will need to employ some acting skills. But this is a specific type of acting. You are not about to play Hamlet but simply experience what it is like to be your partner. By this I mean not just mimicking their expressions but feeling the essence of who they are. If you wonder why acting will help you, think of it this way: acting is the creative ability to stand apart from yourself and feel every aspect of what it is to be another person so that you almost become them. Actors do not become someone else and lose sight of who they are: they reach for deeper places within themselves so that they can empathise with the character and personify them. In your case, by becoming your partner for a short time, you will be able to identify with them as you explore how they might respond and feel about the world.

You do not need your partner to be present for this exercise; in fact it may be preferable if they are not. This experience will help to develop a strong psychic bond as you merge with them, connecting with their spirit within.

Acting out your partner's essence

Find a quiet place and relax. Wear comfortable clothes as you may need to move around. Imagine your partner or have a photograph of them in front of you.

Think about your partner and the way they express themselves. Do they frown a lot, peer, or are they always smiling? Move your facial expression into the way your partner's is often set. Think of their body language. How do they hold their head? Do they tilt it to one side or lean slightly backwards? Do they slouch or are they always straight-backed? What are their hand movements like? Do they gesticulate expressively or are they subdued? How do they walk? Do they move languidly or do they have quick jerky movements? All these things are expressions of their character and tell you a lot about who they are. Now focus on your partner's voice. Is it soft and gentle, or loud and brash? How are you feeling now? Are their expressions making you feel more relaxed or are you tensing up? Try to put all these things together and experience their body language and expressions.

Next try to get a feel for what motivates your partner. Are they happy or sad as a person? Extroverted or introverted? Do they seem tense or relaxed? Experience how that might feel.

This may be difficult to do at first, but persevere as the rewards of appreciating another perspective will reap benefits in your deeper understanding of who your partner is. This empathy will build a strong intuitive bond between you.

As you get more familiar with your partner's expressions and the feel of them, this is the time to look at any conflicts or issues that are causing barriers between you. First, ask yourself a question about a problem where you felt you couldn't understand your partner's point of view. For example, 'Why did you overreact about me going out for a drink?' or 'Why didn't you like that house?' Then answer the question you have posed as if you were your partner, without analysing it. Write down your answer and afterwards look at it clearly. You may be surprised at what you have unearthed, but it will help you to understand what your partner feels and build a greater honesty and communication on all levels between you.

You can use this exercise at any time when you feel there is a rift or a conflict that you cannot work out between you. And you can keep experimenting to gain a better understanding. Explore this together and find out whether your partner agrees with your view of their world.

You have worked through a variety of exercises, all of which are designed to enable you to clear away old issues and build a bridge between your higher mind and your partner's. Keep practising them and your intuitive powers will grow stronger and you will create the higher vibration of unconditional love and deepen the bond between you. Remember, this bond is something special and deep, as the exercises enable you to connect with each other on an intuitive energy level through the voice of your spirit. By building up this psychic connection you are developing your relationship from the inside out so that whatever problems arise will not shake our deeper love and faith in each other. Soon it will become a way of life for you as you have the magical tools to remedy any conflict or obstacle that you face together. Remember that the more you use the exercises the quicker change can happen.

Trusting the process

It is crucial that you now employ the fourth technique of trust and allow the process of everything you have undertaken to unfold. Whatever the circumstances, impatience to see results or over-concentration on the outcome is not the response of someone who is attuned to their higher mind. Remember, by focusing on your exercise and then relinquishing control of the outcome is how miracles happen. If you wish to read more about trust then turn to chapter three, page 83.

Moving forward with your relationship

Your intuitive powers are natural and your souls have already invested a great deal of love and learning in each other through the past lives that you have experienced together. Continue to nurture your inherent gift and your relationship will blossom and evolve as you experience more understanding, awareness, wisdom and compassion. These qualities stem from your intuitive self and when you are tuned in to this, you will recognise the potential in your partner and the value of what you are learning from each other. When you argue or experience conflicts it's easy to make judgements and forget the underlying reason for the force that drew you together. Negative judgements and criticism do not stem from your higher mind, but from your limited ego. When our intuitive self is in the driving seat you are able to heal not only your past life issues but bring out a new pattern of living for the eternal future.

There are many other exercises throughout this book that will help develop your relationship. You may have already discovered from the questionnaire that you also have a soul mate link, so your next adventure of the higher mind is to work through those exercises. And whether you have a soul mate link or not, this book is about developing your psychic self, so allow your intuitive sense to come to the fore as you look through the rest of the chapters. Let your sixth sense guide you to any other exercises that will benefit you, and take note of any other information that may help when you read the last chapter. Note any changes in your diary. I have great faith that you will be amazed at the difference in your relationship.

Continue working on your powerful past life connection and never forget how strongly you are both interlinked in your mutual history. This will remind you of the importance of the love and insight that you bring to your relationship today. Your psychic powers will keep the incredible spark between you alive and give you a launch pad into a golden future of magical adventures.

6 THE PRIMAL SEXUAL CONNECTION

A RELATIONSHIP BASED ON THE MAGNETIC ATTRACTION OF SEXUAL CHEMISTRY

We must not be enemies. Though passion may have strained, it must not break our bonds of affection . . .

ABRAHAM LINCOLN, 1809–65, FORMER US PRESIDENT

Here we turn to the highly charged attraction of the sexual bond. For any of you who are unsure, this is the feeling of lust at first sight which fires up the senses. But rest assured, despite being a purely sexual connection this potent energy has the power to transform you and your relationship into a powerful psychic and spiritual union.

This connection can often cause pain and suffering when we don't learn to harness its fiery energy. Some of you may have experienced the effects of this: the habitual rollercoaster of endless conflicts and reconciliations that bring out heated emotions of lust and jealousy, anger and confusion. Or could it be that your partnership defies all reason as you have a strong attraction to someone with whom you share no emotional or intellectual affinity? The positive side of this connection is that you could be enjoying ongoing passionate relations with your partner, which means you still feel love and lust in equal measure. Whatever the nature of your relationship now, you can learn how to use the sizzling chemistry between you to discover a deeper connection and build on a higher spiritual passion.

Having discovered your strengths and weaknesses through the questionnaire, you can resolve conflicts, gain insight and build empathy. Even if you have an intense physical relationship which is mostly blissful, you can develop the sexual dynamic by learning about your chakras and using the transformative effects of tantric sex to build on that potent desire. By using the four techniques you can channel and focus your psychic energy, gaining awareness and using your imagination and dreams to turn up the heat on the spark you both share and inflame not only your body and your mutual emotions but also your hearts.

What is the primal sexual connection?

A primal sexual link is when you experience the strong impact of sexual magnetism with a partner. This differs from a karmic past life link and soul mate connection in that this bond is fuelled primarily by a sexual force. Although you can experience a strong sexual attraction with past lives and a soul mate there is always a sense of recognition and a strong connection on other levels.

In some ways it is a straightforward attraction. You may not have any other kind of rapport with your partner, and they may be someone who is not your physical type yet the pull between you is compelling and intense. But forget all the talk of pheromones and hormones. When you experience that rush of lust, those elements are triggered because you are responding to similar thought energy within each other, whether a recognition of mutual sexual proclivities or a similar emotional history. This recognition awakens desire and activates the brain to provoke all the other biological functions such as hormones and those sexy brain chemicals.

However, this primal link is about more than just fancying someone in a relaxed way or finding someone aesthetically pleasing. It is that sense of being electrified as soon as your eyes lock together and feeling passionately 'fired up' by someone, which is when you experience the compulsive pull of pure unadulterated lust.

Don't underestimate the sexual link. Just like a roaring fire, you need to ensure that it is built properly with wood-burning logs and not allowed to get out of control and wreak havoc. The force of sexual power is the expression of the pure creative force within and can produce a negative or positive response depending on the energies of the people involved.

For this attraction to last you need to be balanced within your own energy centres – the chakras. Expressing feelings in only a sexual way through your base and splenic chakras will create a concentration of energy in this area if you don't link in any other way, such as intellectually or emotionally. In this case if you are not careful the instantaneous flames of passion can burn out as fast as they started. In a healthy relationship this energy will eventually balance and you will connect on other levels, and develop a strong friendship, or a loving and spiritual bond.

A variety of sexual encounters with unstable people or destructive relationships will also unbalance your chakras, as the residue of energy of an abusive or insecure relationship will leave its trail of influence in the same way as the smell of cigarettes clings to you after you have been around people who smoke. Remember that thoughts and beliefs are energy and have an influence on us even at a distance. Imagine the effects when we are making love. The sexual energy purges your chakras and can bring emotional instability, fear and neediness to the surface if you are already unstable. But if your energy is balanced, you will attract a more balanced partner (see chapter two, page 20 on like attracts like) and this energy has beneficial effects that can make you feel more emotionally content and grounded within yourself and your relationship.

Ultimately, though your sexual energy is a potent and mystical force which, used correctly, has the potential to awaken your psychic powers and enable you to travel to new heights in consciousness.

How your chakras influence your behaviour

Base Chakra

Unbalanced: *you will know that your base chakra is unbalanced if you make unrealistic demands on people and want a lot of attention. Or you may try to manipulate to get your own way.*

Balanced: *you maintain good relationships with people around you and work in a constructive way to get your basic needs met.*

Splenic Chakra

Unbalanced: *sexually this can cause an inability to orgasm, impotence, premature ejaculation or an inability to conceive a child. Emotionally it can mean that you are creatively blocked in which case you might find it hard to come up with ideas or have 'writer's block'. This imbalance can also indicate that you are selfish or arrogant. You may feel insecure, mistrustful of* *others and overly worried about how others see you. Of course you won't experience all of these at once, but, depending on the imbalance, you may be affected in some of these ways.*

Balanced: *you have a healthy understanding of your sexuality and take pleasure in giving and receiving in all aspects of life.*

Solar Plexus Chakra

Unbalanced: *you may be over-critical and judgemental of others. You may also be insecure, constantly seeking approval from others or measuring yourself by other people's standards.*

Balanced: *you are self-sufficient and independent. You set your own standards and commit yourself to meeting them. Essentially, you feel secure and stable within yourself.*

Heart Chakra

Unbalanced: *this imbalance reveals itself in jealousy, possessiveness, paranoia and manipulative behaviour. You may try to control others emotionally to get what you want. There may also be an increase in feelings of insecurity, self-doubt, unstable behaviour and self-punishment.*

Balanced: *you feel secure in matters of the heart. You love yourself and others in a healthy way. You don't feel the need to prove yourself or manipulate. You are trusting and open.*

Throat Chakra

Unbalanced: *imbalance reveals itself in extreme behaviour. You may be domineering, trying to control others by imposing your views on them. Equally, you may be submissive or passive,* *seeking to manipulate through a display of weakness. Both types of behaviour seek to control.*

Balanced: *you are able to communicate clearly and honestly how you feel. In other words you speak your truth. You trust that your partner will hear your point of view and take it seriously.*

Brow Chakra

Unbalanced: *you may be over-sensitive, anxious or have a tendency to blow things out of proportion. You may also be insensitive to others and find it hard to empathise with them. You will struggle to use your intuition or follow your hunches.*

Balanced: *you find it easy to use your intuition and have a balanced perception of things. You empathise easily with others and generally have insight, wisdom and good judgement of situations.*

Crown Chakra

Unbalanced: *this can mean that you live in a Pollyanna world where you see everything through rose-coloured glasses. You may be interested in developing your intuition or spiritual pursuits but find it hard to apply them practically to your life. Equally, it can mean the opposite and you may be blinkered to anything involving spiritual truth. This imbalance may reveal a denial of your inner self and a desire to accept only rational, everyday things that can be proved.*

Balanced: *you are comfortable with your spirituality and have had many spiritual experiences. You are creative and accept and nurture your inner self. You understand your purpose for being here and what you are meant to do.*

Your Primal Partner

If you can't stand the heat, then you really do need to stay out of the kitchen, bedroom or any other living area. If you are confused by what I mean here then you are reading the wrong chapter. For those of you who have discovered that you have a primal sexual connection you will realise why this phrase was made for you, as you understand the compelling nature of this passionate magnetism all too well. You know how addictive and intense it feels as your hormones are sent into overdrive. And how your mind is in a whirl as all sense of logic is lost in the moment.

Perhaps you have seen the devastation this fiery energy can cause if it is not handled correctly and how it can blind you to reason. You may have wondered how something so intense could burn out so quickly. Perhaps you quickly discovered that despite this overwhelming passion, you had little common ground and possibly no mental rapport. Or are you one of the lucky ones who have kept this passion burning as your relationship has matured into something deeper and more long-lasting?

However long your relationship lasted you could well have had many intuitive experiences, as the surge of creative sexual force awakens psychic energy. It is this profound force that you need to harness and develop to create a healthy, balanced relationship that stems from a deeper core of love. Through the exercises in this chapter you can use your higher mind to plug you into your inner voice and allow intuition to be the guiding force in your relationship. You will then create an inner stability that can survive any crisis as well as enjoy a potent connection between you that will give you a heightened experience of love and bonding.

Let's focus on a constructive example of the primal sexual

connection. In the following example Nicola, a city executive, experienced instant lust at first sight with her partner Paul. What she thought would be a casual fling became a strong, supportive relationship and they have remained together for over three years, despite facing unforeseeable challenges that would change their lives.

Nicola's story: achieving happiness

Nicola, thirty-nine, met her partner Paul, twenty-seven, at a club in London. The club was tightly packed and bustling with revellers, but as soon as their eyes met they felt an immediate mutual desire which seemed to cross over the normal dating rules. As Nicola danced Paul pulled her towards him, and they kissed as they danced together provocatively. There was no romantic star-struck wonderment between them yet their attraction seemed completely natural. It was evident – no words were needed – that they would indeed spend the night together.

They went back to his flat and both tore off their clothes in a frenzy. According to Nicola it was one of the wildest nights she had ever experienced – and, as she proclaims, she was no Mary Poppins.

Nicola continues, 'The next morning we chatted in a relaxed way and he walked me home which fortunately was only ten minutes away.

'I remembered thinking, Wow, what a night to remember but I'll probably never see him again.'

She gave him her number, not expecting a call but hopeful that they might get together again casually for another hot night.

Three weeks later, she got a phone call. This time he came straight to her house and it was an immediate race to the bedroom without any social niceties.

'It was obvious from the start', says Nicola, 'that despite a

twelve-year age gap, we completely gelled on a sexual level. The prime interest was totally animal and the chemistry between us literally seemed to sizzle. There was no great meeting of minds but our chit-chat was friendly enough.

'After that there were never any formal arrangements made or dates. And certainly no wooing campaign. It was literally very spontaneous and of the moment: he would ring every few days and I didn't think that it would ever be any more than just an extended one-night stand. Great fun, wild passion, but totally casual.

'In many ways we were poles apart. I liked opera, dining out and was in the corporate industry running my own advertising business. He, on the other hand, liked reggae music, fast food and was more of a blue-collar worker. But I never minded not being taken out or attending a classical concert. I can do that with friends, but on the other hand what he gave me in sheer unadulterated lust, I couldn't get from my friends.'

It was evident they were an unlikely combination, yet pulled together like magnets, with a flurry of wild primitive energy creating sparks between them.

As time ticked by, although there was no intellectual rapport, they developed a relationship that was both intensely sexual and mutually supportive.

'I found that although we met in this way,' continues Nicola, 'he was one of the most caring and responsible individuals that I had ever met. It was as if the flurry of sexual activity between us seemed to connect us on a deeper level. Often Paul would begin to express his emotions when we made love and say how he felt, which he never did at any other time. Over a period of time a real feeling of cherishing each other came to the fore and suddenly at the core of our passion was real deep love. This was a great support to me as at that time I was made bankrupt and my

company fell apart. I got very depressed but Paul was the one who was always talking me through things and helping me out in practical ways by moving furniture, decorating and helping me find a new house to live in. You could never call him highbrow or say his head was in the clouds like previous lovers, yet he had all the earthy elements of practicality, steadfastness and diligence.

'As the relationship began on such a spontaneous level we both continued along those lines. We both got together feeling free to do so without expectations. The growing affection between us meant I never felt insecure and never pressurised him or expected him to be a certain way. He always says how much he appreciates that I don't hound him or make demands. That freedom and spontaneity is what, I believe, keeps us together and created such a strong bond. We value each other for who we are and not an ideal that we aspire to be.'

This relationship shows that, despite starting on a purely sexual link, they developed their partnership into a supportive, loving friendship. When Nicola was made bankrupt, Paul showed himself to be more than just a sexual liaison and became one of the most supportive partners Nicola says she has ever had. Because it was such an instant sexual bond, with no expectations or demands made, they gave their relationship time to grow into something worth while.

Your Primal Potential

When you and your partner are both connected to your intuition, you can bring out your spiritual potential as well as developing a powerful and loving bond. One of the ways of developing this psychic connection between you and your lover is to awaken the primitive power of Kundalini, the power of pure desire within us. It is our sacred life force where psychic gifts, inspiration, creativity and revelation originate and it is often awakened through tantric sex. Although lovers with any type of connection can raise Kundalini through tantric sex, those with a strong sexual energy have a head start. With so much fiery passion you are driven with an insatiable desire to make love as often as possible, which means you have the perfect opportunity to focus this force. We will explore this energy force and tantric sex in more detail in the second exercise of this chapter.

All strong sexual desire is a manifestation of a deeper desire to unite spiritually, whether we know it or not. This is why the powerful feeling of lust can lead some of you to have psychic experiences right from the start of your union. Perhaps you felt that your lover was about to ring you and then picked up the phone to find them on the end of the line; or you intuitively knew when they were thinking of you.

By focusing this energy through the sexual act you can stabilise the heat between you to stop it burning out and causing any instability. Problems and insecurity can occur when you have a strong sexual desire but no other connection, particularly if you have imbalances within your chakras, as the powerful sexual energy will purge your energy points and bring issues to the surface to be cleansed. This can create a whole host of emotional reactions from paranoia to jealousy and obsessiveness. (See box on page 182.)

However, connecting with your intuitive power produces incredible results as it evokes a transforming, magical influence on you and your relationship. You will both feel an equilibrium and harmony within yourselves and you will therefore become more trusting, honest and open, which is essential if you want your partnership to stand the test of time. As a result you won't be so affected by jealousy and warped perceptions of your partner, which make you critical and judgemental. You will experience a clearer mind so when conflicts arise you won't need to manipulate or score points to win an argument. There will be an empathy with what your partner is trying to express and you will see behind their personality to the inner person. You can then communicate more honestly but without hostility, simply because you trust that your partner is taking on board what you are saying. Above all, because you are nurturing your own intuitive self you will feel more at peace and therefore respond from a place of love and contentment, which creates reassurance and appreciation within your relationship. Relationships flounder when we respond from our egos and focus on the negative. Intuition taps you in to your higher mind so that you feel positive and connected with your partner on much deeper levels.

Let's look at the way you responded to the questionnaire and the weaknesses in your union that may have been revealed. Answers you gave to specific questions illuminate how you feel within your relationship. If you have more than one yes answer in the destructive category there is evidence that your relationship is damaging and negative and needs to be rectified.

Destructive Tendencies

If the questionnaire revealed negative elements in your relationship, this chapter will help you to develop your intuitive powers to channel your potential.

If you are serious about developing your psychic powers to strengthen your partnership bond, you must learn to respect and honour the sexual act if you are to understand its impact on your emotional and psychic health.

Sex can be a great healing tool within a close relationship, but some sexual encounters with destructive or unbalanced people can leave a negative impact on your auric field, akin to energy contamination. So casual one-night stands or even making love for years with a violent and destructive partner can influence your psychological and emotional health, making you feel insecure and unstable.

When we make love, however casual the acquaintance, it is much more than a physical act. Our souls, spirits and auras merge with each other and link with our mind and body. With each sexual liaison, even if it's a one-night stand, we create cords of light that connect us to the other person through our second chakras. These cords remain connected throughout our lives. And they are often the reason why insecurities and emotions are brought to the surface during and after sex, whether old emotional wounds resurfacing, a sense of vulnerability, feelings of abandonment, disgust or feeling unsettled. It's no wonder some people feel strange the morning after an encounter. You have the remnants of someone else's energy merging with yours as well as being tied to them through an energetic cord of light.

Your answers to specific questions revealed areas of conflict and tension between you, and you may be affected on an energy level by your current or previous partners. The quiz was a mirror for what you already knew by the way you both respond to each other. Take an objective overview of the emotional dynamic between you. If you are always battling over issues, or feel jealous, angry or hurt you know that these are problems that need to be resolved in order to enjoy the kind of communication you both deserve. Perhaps you are on a habitual rollercoaster where you are a slave to endless fights that lead to passionate reunions. Or maybe the sexual chemistry between you seems to have evaporated. Be truthful and don't delude yourself that sex will always be the solution or create solidarity between you. There needs to be emotional and spiritual depth, understanding and compassion between you too.

Liberation comes from harnessing your sexual energy. When we learn to contain our more basic instincts we can understand how to awaken our deeper intuitive force. Whatever the condition of your relationship, as you work through these specific exercises and focus your psychic power on your union, you will be clearing out your aura and allowing your intuition to connect you with your finer feelings of patience, affection and understanding. As a result, you will naturally feel more discriminate and committed to your partner and open up a reservoir of unconditional love and healing that can transform your relationship.

Feelings of Disconnection

If the questionnaire illuminated a feeling of detachment or isolation in your relationship there may be several reasons why this has happened.

You may have remained on a base sexual level and not connected properly on other levels. Although you might have begun with a powerful sexual feeling that made you feel connected, you need to build and balance your sexual energy if you want your relationship to blossom and grow. A partnership cannot be completely fulfilling or exciting when it is only one-dimensional. It is easy to fall into the trap of believing you are a sexual being and that honest communication or understanding on a deeper level isn't important. You will end up as strangers who can express their feelings in only one way.

Or perhaps passion has brought insecurities to the surface and instead of communicating them honestly, they are festering inside you. You will become moody and distant if you don't express how you feel, and this discontent could affect you emotionally and physically, creating ill health or depression.

The energy cords that bind you and your partner together through your chakras will be damaged, twisted or embedded, revealing the unhealthy connection in your relationship. Numerous past sexual encounters will also reflect in the cords and prevent healthy connections in a present relationship, which could mean you feel constantly restless and unable to commit, or you could attract the wrong partner to you, someone who is uncommitted and unstable. In contrast, strong loving sexual relations create strong beautiful cords of light, which bestow a clearer sense of your own identity.

Clearing the air and expressing how you feel can help you both to see each other anew and rekindle the fire in your love lives. Open, honest communication clears out negative suppressed energies and therefore helps you feel more connected to each other so that you both feel passionate again. But remember to communicate calmly and not just rage at or criticise your partner. Otherwise your candid feelings won't serve you or your relationship and you will only create more conflicts.

Equally, it may be time to recognise that there has to be more to a relationship than lust. A sexually based relationship can be fun for a while until you feel used, empty or bored. And to any sex addicts reading this book, I'm afraid that promiscuous behaviour can destabilise you and will distance you from your emotions.

You need to tap in to the spirit of your partner, which can be a huge adventure and means diving beneath the physical surface and seeing your sexual expression as a reflection of the many different facets you both have. After all, how you think and feel influences the way you make love. Learning about your partner on all levels doesn't have to be intense and serious. Even if you think you know everything about them, you never really stop discovering new things. So remain a student of love. You can reignite that passion by tapping in to your intuitive self and let it take you to a new experience of communication.

Knowing when it's time to move on.

It's time to go if you feel that your relationship is destructive and brings out the worst in you both. If you are deeply unhappy it will be difficult to find the positive energy to turn things around, and both you and your partner have to strive for a positive outcome. Using the psychic exercises to reconnect you to a deeper awareness and understanding takes effort and persistence. If you feel that communication between you is impossible or that your life is more of a battleground than a playground, then it could be time to move on.

You and your partner should bring out the best in each other not the worst, otherwise you will stagnate and create more conflicts. Continual battles will not allow you to grow or teach you anything. Such a relationship will simply damage you both. There must be a resolution to understand and provide insight as to why these negative reactions recur and how to focus on a bigger picture.

A link with your intuitive self will enable you to see beyond your partner's persona and realise that you want more from your relationship than spent passion. You need to rise to the potential of a supportive and loving relationship, have no expectations and stop the negative cycle of knee-jerk reactions. Otherwise you could be frozen in time with an unsupportive lover, feeling deeply resentful and unfulfilled. If you know that your relationship is at an end and you find the courage to move forward you have the opportunity to find love with someone with whom you can share the many dimensions of yourself.

Understanding and Healing Your Primal Connection

Once you have recognised the downside of your relationship, in order to progress, you must decide whether to reignite the spark between you and allow it to transmute so you deepen your connection and allow it to become a fire in your heart. If you are willing then begin the series of exercises that will awaken your intuition and create a passionately loving bond between you.

You are now going to progress to the second and third techniques which will help you to focus your mind and utilise your imaginative skills. Whatever issues you need to resolve, whether conflicts, sexual problems, self-esteem or boredom, know that you can overcome them and enjoy a relationship that fulfils both of you on deeper levels.

The first exercise is crucial as it is designed to clear out negative emotions from your chakra energy points and enable you to feel more balanced and centred so you can bring your imaginative powers into play. Sexual energy can create unsettlement and make you feel insecure if you feel unstable within yourself. A cycle of drama and conflict or denial and stress in a relationship will certainly knock your chakras out of kilter, as negative thoughts, emotions and beliefs will affect these energy points adversely. This breathing exercise gives you an opportunity to ensure your chakras are functioning correctly and eliminate toxic emotional waste. Your cleared chakras will then allow the cords that connect you and your partner to be strengthened and cleansed.

Once you are rid of some of your negative energies you will

feel more connected to the frequency of the earth's magnetic field which resonates with the higher vibration of intuition and unconditional love. By achieving this you will feel less stressed and reactive, as any blocked energy flows freely again. This means you will feel more in tune with your own feelings and those of your partner as you are in the perfect alpha state to create a powerful vision of how you want your relationship to be. You will then be fully prepared to take your relationship forward to the next stage as you gain further insight into the primal sexual connection and embark on awakening Kundalini energy through tantric sex.

Cleanse and Rebalance Your Chakras

This exercise is based on a breathing technique which draws up the energy of the earth through your chakras and helps them to become more balanced by clearing them of negative energy.

First, light some candles and draw your curtains to give you privacy and create a calming atmosphere. Then practise inhaling into your belly instead of into your chest. If you do yoga, you may be used to this type of breathing, but otherwise it may take some practice. Keep breathing into this area and then exhale. It may help to put your fingers on your stomach, so you can keep redirecting your breath there. You should be able to see your belly rise and fall with each breath.

Stand with your feet about three feet apart and keep your back straight. Place the tips of your fingers once again over your stomach area. Take a deep breath into your stomach and focus your mind on the centre of your stomach and make it hot. If you visualise this heat properly, you will start to feel warm. Visualise your breath being drawn up from the core of the earth. Imagine how hot the core of the earth would be, so visualise this breath as being warm, hold for ten seconds and then slowly breathe out. Do this three more times, ensuring that you inhale deeply from the earth into your stomach and then slowly exhale.

Now you are going to breathe into each of your chakras. Keep your legs slightly bent if you can, but if you feel uncomfortable then simply stand up straight. It is more important for you to be comfortable and relaxed.

Start with the base chakra at the bottom of the spine. Inhale deeply into this chakra, putting your hands on the area to help you focus as if your breath is coming from the core of the earth. Feel this area expanding with warm earth energy, as if it were a lung. Hold for ten seconds and then slowly exhale.

Then breathe into the splenic chakra located in the small of the back. Put your fingers on the front part of this area and once again breathe from the earth into the chakra and visualise that area expanding like a lung, then slowly exhale.

Move up to the third solar plexus chakra, place your fingers on the stomach area and inhale deeply, visualise your stomach expanding with air and slowly breathe out.

Breathe into the fourth heart chakra in the centre of your chest and place your fingers there to sense where you should feel the breath and imagine it expanding, then slowly exhale.

Move up to the fifth throat chakra and concentrate, as you may need to focus to imagine inhaling the earth energy into your throat. See your throat expanding like a lung in your mind's eye and then slowly exhale.

Focus your breath now into your sixth chakra located in the third eye area in the centre of your brow and see this small area expand with air and breathe out.

Lastly, breathe into your seventh crown chakra on the top of your head. The crown chakra is not a chakra in the same way as the others, but an opening where energy can enter and leave the body. For this one just imagine breathing the warm earth energy into the top part of your scalp and visualise that area expanding.

Now that you have breathed into all seven energy centres, I want you to visualise the outcome of what you want to achieve in your relationship or with a new partner. (Refer back to chapter three, page 74 if you want to be reminded how to do this.) Recreate a loving picture of you both in the present, making it as realistic as possible, using all your senses, and say an affirmation as if it is happening now such as, 'My partner and I are loving and secure together.' You feel deeply relaxed and cleansed, so this will help you to project your future reality and allow your mind to absorb it as a belief. Have implicit trust that it will happen.

Finally, breathe again from the core of the earth but this time imagine the energy moving all the way up your spine and then exhale through your heart chakra in the centre of your chest. Do this twice more.

Next visualise a white laser beam of light coming through the crown of your head, down your spine and through the centre of your body to the soles of your feet and extending down deeply into the core of the earth, making you feel totally secure.

You should feel cleaner and lighter, as this process will have helped to cleanse and harmonise your chakras from any residue left over from destructive or negative relationships past and present. You will know if it has worked, because you will feel 'different', although the experience will vary for everyone.

What have you achieved

You have cleansed and rebalanced your chakras, bringing any old conflicts to the surface and replaced your negative energies with a positive vision of what you want to achieve. Did you find it easy to breathe into each chakra? If you are not used to breathing in this way, then practise and it will feel more comfortable. Even if you cannot manage breathing in the right way, do persist with the exercise as the very intent of actively cleansing your chakras will none the less have a positive effect and help them to function more efficiently; which in turn will help you feel centred and energised. Initially, though, the cleansing process may make you feel melancholy, irritable, tired or angry. If you do, don't be alarmed as these are simply repressed feelings that have come to the surface to be released. Acknowledge them by saying 'thank you' in your mind, which will integrate the lesson they have taught you on an energy level, and you can let them go. It is crucial that you clear your mind energy and aura of toxic, negative issues so that you begin from a new perspective and fresh ground and your relationship can flourish.

The visualisation that came after you had breathed into your chakras was perfectly timed to help your progress. Your frequency of vibration was heightened and in this alpha state you were able to create your reality of how ideally you want your relationship to be. This altered mind state enables your subconscious to absorb fully your positive vision as a new belief without any limited thoughts obstructing your progress. This has paved the way for you to feel more liberated within yourself from any emotional baggage cluttering up your energy field and you will see your partner with a renewed perspective. You will send out loving vibrations that your loved one will unconsciously pick up on and this will make you feel closer to one another. To put this in context, read what happened when a couple allowed their passion to turn into conflicts and destroy their relationship.

Sam's story: the break-up

When Sam, a journalist, and Jane, a secretary, met through work it was pure sexual chemistry. Their eyes seemed to lock and Sam confessed that there was an electrifying frisson between them. They kissed frenziedly within an hour of accidentally bumping into each other in the corridor, and were in bed together that night. They described a feeling of overpowering lust.

Afterwards they couldn't keep their hands off each other but on another level they always seemed to know instantly when the other person was thinking of them. Jane would sense if Sam was trying to contact her, switch the computer on and find an e-mail waiting. Or he'd ring just as she was about to pick up the phone. Even their emotions were filtering through. If she felt sad, he'd ring to see if she was okay because he felt suddenly worried. Sam knew that there was no intellectual bond and in fact they didn't do much talking. There wasn't anything to say. It was more like he'd be round in ten minutes and they'd tumble into bed. Though Sam agreed that there were, of course, romantic gestures and he would buy little gifts and pick her up from work. It was affectionate, free from commitment and happy. Sadly, though, their fun wasn't to last and the couple split up within a few months.

Soon they were rowing over little things, which became more and more volatile. Small problems were inflated into huge conflicts as Sam was accused of chatting up other women or Jane was deemed to be jealous and a flirt. At first they thought their possessiveness a sign of love, but it then ricocheted into endless fights that they partly enjoyed because they ended in a passionate making-up. Soon they were in a routine of conflict and reconciliation and they both felt tired and stressed. Their psychic receptors began to wane. The passion was still there but it was like a spectre looming over them as their dream turned into a living nightmare.

Their relationship ended badly with both feeling exhausted and angry.

This couple are the perfect example of what happens when you allow passion to fly out of control and become dependent on creating more fire through conflict and fighting. While this may seem exciting for a while, eventually it will exhaust you and make you physically ill and mentally unstable. It's all too easy to choose conflict as a way of firing up your relationship. But it's a short-term futile solution that won't help either of you to understand yourselves or each other. Eventually the energy between you becomes destructive or simply fizzles out.

Had they known about the transformative psychic techniques the outcome of this couple's relationship could have been quite different. By connecting to their intuition they would have continued to feel the positive energy flowing between them, instead of allowing the passion to overtake them and grow destructive. They could have freed themselves of any negative tension that had built up between them by using the chakra breathing exercise and focused on a positive vision of what they wanted to achieve. And they would have felt more connected to each other by expressing their sexual energy through tantric sex so that their finer qualities could have come to the fore. The effects of this would have been that they would have responded emphatically to each other when faced with conflicts or disagreements instead of giving knee-jerk reactions.

When we are balanced and centred within ourselves we relate more harmoniously to our loved ones. But a powerfully charged sexual relationship alone will unbalance us if none of our other needs are being met.

* * *

To ensure that we heighten our intuitive powers in the right way to dissolve any conflicts in a partnership we will focus on harnessing the higher vibrations of our sexual energy. In the following exercise you will discover that with controlled practice you can create a deep and powerful psychic bond within your relationship. Controlling and experiencing our sexuality on a higher level of consciousness is one of the ways in which we can contact the powerful, sacred force within us, called Kundalini. Awakening Kundalini in the sexual act is like alchemy. It can transform your relationship in many ways and on many levels. Whatever conflicts or difficulties you have experienced you can create a magnetised loving harmony and resonance between you. Your cords of connection between your chakras will strengthen and you will feel more at one. This interconnectedness will engender a profound mind-to-mind link which means telepathy between you can occur even at a distance. And as you feel more psychically connected you will benefit from a more satisfying sex life that can bring a sense of physical, mental and spiritual union. The empathy between you will increase as you become more in tune with each other's feelings, and you will feel a sense of uplift and centred tranquillity. Mastering your Kundalini force will evolve you into a supernatural lover, in control of your powerful sexual energy, which will help you create the relationship you always dreamed of.

Using Kundalini energy to strengthen your relationship

As I mentioned earlier by channelling the powerful sexual force between you and your partner you can awaken a mystical energy source known as Kundalini. In the following exercise we will focus on tantric sex and how you can awaken this energy to connect more profoundly with your partner and experience a powerful telepathic resonance.

What is Kundalini? It is a potent source of energy which lies dormant in our sacrum in the base of our spine (our base chakra). It is often symbolised in Eastern philosophy as the fiery serpent which when awakened uncoils and rises up like a white fluid light and flows through each of the six chakras until it reaches the crown chakra.

It is said that when you feel the full impact of Kundalini you experience enlightenment, and it has been likened to an explosion of joy, a feeling of heat moving through your spine or a cool breeze that flows over the top of your head.

This energy also has a dramatic influence. As Kundalini moves through the chakras like a powerful laser it purges any old emotional issues or subconscious fears, bringing them to the surface to be cleared away. Your chakras are likened to spinning wheels of energy, and as the force enters each chakra, it increases the spin, which expels toxins. When the chakra is cleared, it raises the energy frequency of that point. Every repressed emotion or painful memory trapped within each chakra is purged so that the energy can flow freely again. So although the experience can be blissful, the cleansing process can also evoke a temporary reaction called 'kriyas' which can make you laugh or cry within minutes, or bring deeply repressed emotions to the surface as you experience bliss, joy, terror or rage.

The release of old negative energies means that we experience our relationships with a new level of clarity and joy that was once unimaginable.

Strengthening Your Connection through Tantric Sex

Tantric sex is one of the ways in which Kundalini can be raised. I must point out that the subject of tantric sex is extensive and a way of life for many people. Here I can only give you some basic knowledge which can help you to develop your psychic energy, raise Kundalini and strengthen your relationship.

The sacred and ancient art of tantric sex (which is a form of yoga) first emerged around AD 600 in Indian history and the teachings were embodied in the scriptures. However historians believe that tantra's roots reach back into pre-Aryan times where mystical fertility cults worshipped the female power of regeneration. This philosophy regards sexual energy as sacred and something that is worthy of worship and respect rather than to be frittered away.

The word tantra *is Sanskrit and means 'expansion'. And expansion of your consciousness within your sexual expression is what this yoga aims to teach. The basis of these Eastern teachings is control of the orgasmic state in sexual intercourse. Tantric teachers believe that control of an orgasm brings focused strength and mastery of your sexual energy as you are maintaining this force at its height of maximum power. The results are considered life-enhancing. Tantric expert Dinu Roman claims, 'A man who retains his ejaculatory seed can stay powerful and strong, both physically and mentally. He can keep his stamina up to a very old age and can stay virile practically until he dies.'*

Regular sexual intercourse can awaken Kundalini but only if it is intense and lasts for a long time. This doesn't mean coming back from a party, drunk, and indulging in hours of sex. Contrary to conventional beliefs, habitual sexual intercourse does not necessarily create intimacy or induce loving feelings if it is done with a mechanical complacent attitude or lack of respect for a partner.

For Kundalini to rise, both lovers need to have developed their higher minds and approach the sexual act with sensitivity and awareness of each other's sexual energy. The philosophy is to honour and respect your partner as a cohort in a sensory adventure. Raising Kundalini through tantric sex is about raising pure consciousness and has nothing to do with base desires.

Preparation, patience and persistence are the key words for ensuring maximum benefits from tantric sex.

The Tantra Rules for Enlightened Love

First of all prepare a cosy den that will inspire meditative eroticism and transform your bedroom into a calming, sensual place. Ensure that it is tidy, as you are not distracted by clutter, and comfortably warm. Switch off your telephone, close your curtains and light some candles, scattering them around the room on windowsills, shelves and tables. Or if you wish you can use subtle lighting. A violet light stimulates feminine sexual energy and a red light activates male energy. Invigorate your senses by burning incense such as a heady musk, sandalwood or an evocative jasmine. Or burn an aromatic oil such as patchouli or ylang-ylang. Have some scented massage oil to hand. Play some background music, opera, classical, African or South American music, or, if you prefer, the sounds of nature or the ocean. Music is great for blocking out background noise, inspiring you and helping to focus your mind.

Once you have created a sensual and inspiring atmosphere,

take a warm bath together to destress and freshen your body and mind from the day. Bathing is the perfect way to change a mood and create a reflective frame of mind. Once again, light some candles and have some background music in the bathroom to relax you. Take this time to focus on each other and empty your mind of all worldly thoughts. This is a period of shared tranquillity and sensuality to reconnect with a deeper level of communication.

After your bath sit in front of each other in your prepared room naked, or, if you prefer, in loose clothing. Prepare your mind that you will be re-educating your concept of sex. Remain aware that the ultimate aim in tantra is to control the orgasmic state. But this time you will not seek to end in any normal sexual release but instead to focus on the sensuality between you both. If you find this difficult to get your head around perhaps for the first few times you should forget about sexual intercourse and concentrate only on a sensual communication.

Begin by synchronising with your partner's breathing rhythm, mirroring the way you both inhale and exhale while gazing into each other's eyes. Continue for as long as you wish until you become attuned to each other's body language and feel yourself become an extension of the other. This brings a feeling of affinity and intimacy.

Slowly touch each other. Focus on how your sexual energy feels and how it affects your body and be aware of your partner's responses. Feel how your breath rises and falls and hear and feel your heart beating and any other sensations of hot or cold. The mood should be meditative and reflective. Continue to focus on the sensuality between you and your partner then massage each other with scented oils, preferably a pure essential oil mixed with a carrier oil. A sexually stimulating scent is sandalwood or ylang-

ylang, or for a gentler effect use geranium or bergamot. Be aware of the sensuality in your movements.

When you are comfortable expressing yourself in this way, begin to make love if you wish, but remain aware of the erotic energy running through you. As the energy transmitted through lovemaking begins to build, instead of progressing to orgasm in the normal way, the man doesn't ejaculate and the woman controls her orgasm. Instead of your sexual energy being released, it is transformed and builds into an overpowering euphoria that leaves you with a long-lasting feeling of liberation and joy. When you experience this feeling, it is a sure sign that Kundalini has been awakened.

With regular practice and the right state of mind this form of yoga can bring a balance to your sexuality through the integration of the feminine intuitive yin energy and the masculine pragmatic yang force. You have come a long way in becoming heightened lovers. You have already cleared your chakras and created a vision of the way you want your relationship to be. You have built a stronger connection with each other's higher minds and with each other, creating a spiritual, psychic and emotional bond that gives a feeling of completion and will heighten all your paranormal powers of telepathy and intuition, helping creativity to flow. You can both experience more expansive and powerful orgasms that transcend the physical and evoke a spiritual awakening. With more balance to your energy you learn to react consciously towards your partner, with control and awareness, rather than just reacting blindly from your own viewpoint. Over a period of time a higher intuitive communication can occur between you as you become more attuned to each other's thoughts and feelings. This brings about a deeper feeling of empathy and trust, being able to understand each other's innermost feelings even from a great distance.

Questions to ask yourself

1 Were you able to tune in to each other and feel more bonded? If not, it could be there are issues between you, whether personal or work-related or the effects of stress in other areas of your life, that are blocking you. Keep practising and relaxing with each other to refocus on non-verbal communication and re-establish a connection. Couples can often become virtual strangers despite seeing each other every day and having regular sex if they are switched off to each other.

2 Did you feel frustrated with the lack of orgasm release? Tantra doesn't have to be an everyday event, which could turn into an ordeal. You can continue having a normal sex life, but when it comes to tantric sex, you are creating a time for sacred sex. Take your time and don't proceed to intercourse until you are relaxed and comfortable being intimate with each other. You are changing the pattern of the way you normally make love and refocusing on intimacy rather than just a release of sexual tension. It is important for you to connect and learn to play with your sexual energy in order to gain mastery over it. The results are worth striving for as not only are they life-enhancing but you and your partner will have a deep spiritual connection of unconditional love to celebrate.

You have now worked through two important exercises, which will ignite your psychic powers as well as fan the flames of your passion and take you to a deeper and more loving relationship.

You now have a heightened ability to tune in to your partner and are equipped with exercises to increase love and harmony and eliminate conflicts. Pursue the development of your higher mind regularly and your supernatural powers as well as the bond with your partner will flourish. Then you can use your primal power to overcome any conflict and create the long-lasting love that you both deserve.

The Psychic Power of Erotic Dreaming

As you continue with these powerful exercises, deep and extensive cleansing within your chakras and your auric field will take place. Some old thoughts, emotions and beliefs will naturally come to the surface to be released.

Repressed sexual desires are deeply embedded in the psyche and when they are cleared they often come to the surface in the form of an erotic dream. Anything that remains repressed or you are in denial about will cause a block and although it is not always a good idea to act everything out, your dreams and fantasies are a way of dealing with your primal urges. By clearing out your emotional and psychological junk, you are able to move closer to your partner to experience a deeper, more fulfilling intimacy.

Use this opportunity to meet up and experience connecting with each other in your dream state. You will develop a stronger psychic bond and experience a more profound sexual connection. Start by creating a dream diary as illustrated in chapter four on soul mates, page 128.

Before you go to sleep, think about meeting your partner in your dreams in a specific place. Focus on the sexual energy between you, and that you want to experience the connection of sexual spirituality. This will work even more powerfully if you and your partner discuss before you go to sleep where you want to meet and the experience you want to have. If you are both willing write down your desire to express your spiritual and sexual energy to create a strong bond. Or you can do this alone. Writing it down helps to clarify your thoughts and create more awareness in your subconscious mind.

Next visualise where you are meeting your partner, perhaps in a comfortable, sensual room, and imagine making love to them and your mutual feelings of erotic rapture. You may have to practise this several times for it to seep into your dream state. But it should happen more easily if you are already experiencing tantric sex and opening up your psychic awareness through other exercises.

Write down any dreams you have immediately on waking and be sure to take note of the atmosphere of the dream as well as any feelings you have. Your dream state is a wonderful way to resolve sexual and emotional issues and overcome conflicts between you and your partner – even if you don't manage to meet up. Some of your issues may even be unconscious and your dreams will bring them to the surface so that you release them. The more developed your psychic awareness, the clearer your dreams will be. You can still interpret a confusing dream which is cloaked in symbolism but it is a sign that you are not connecting with your higher mind. As you develop your psychic awareness your dreams will become more straightforward and uncomplicated.

Sometimes you can literally dream of making love to a real or fantasy lover and experience a dream orgasm. This can be just a release of sexual tension or an unresolved sexual desire.

Look at what some of the symbols below mean but be aware that the symbol relates to what you asked your dream the night before. The same symbolic sign in a dream about work will mean something quite different from a quest to understand your sexual self. These depictions are examples focused on the primal side of your nature.

Animal Symbolism

Animals are often represented in an archetypal form. A cat represents a free spirit and sexual satisfaction, while horses suggest strength and power. A flying bird can suggest exploring new heights in your sexuality. (Any feelings of flying suggest liberation, sexual ecstasy and release. Or it could be a yearning for freedom and a desire to awaken your sexual self.)

Atmosphere and effects of nature

Often different types of weather are a backdrop to an erotic dream. Dreams of rivers, torrential rain or a stormy sea can all indicate strong emotions and churning sexual arousal. Boiling water can relate to raising the temperature or wanting to heat up your love life.

On the flip side fog, heavy mist or a dense cloud can indicate that you are hiding your true sexual desires from yourself or others. Perhaps you feel uncomfortable with this side of yourself. The chakra exercise earlier in the chapter can help you to rid yourself of old sexual issues and hang-ups that may be festering in your subconscious and blocking you from experiencing true passion.

Miserable rain can symbolise depression or unhappiness and being saturated by rain can indicate feeling overwhelmed and powerless. Thunder and lightning can be a symbol of great passion or great anger. How you feel in the dream will relay the truth.

Nourishment

Food and drink are the perfect symbols of sexual appetite. If you are stuffing yourself with cakes or a huge, delicious meal then you are embarking on a fulfilling sex life or desiring one. The larger and more exotic your dream appetite and spread of food, the more imaginative your sexual hunger. One friend told me of a dream where she got into a taxi and there was a cook in the front passenger seat offering a gourmet meal. Her nieces were there indulging in all that was on offer. In reality she had met a man from overseas and while she felt there was no long-term future in it, she was very attracted and wanted to have fun. The dream indicated a short-lived but expensive trip that would provide her with sexual pleasure. It turned out to be an accurate premonition.

This type of dreaming will help to highlight any issues that need resolving within your partnership and help harness the telepathy between you. If it doesn't work the first time, don't worry, keep practising. The mind is very good at absorbing repeated instructions and these will soon filter through to your dream state. Remember to relax and be patient. Intuition flows when you view your development process as an enjoyable adventure.

Trust

You now need to implement the fourth technique of trust. Just like emotion, intuition is invisible to the eye, but we know that it exists by how we feel. Trusting that your psychic work will have an effect is essential for you to double its effectiveness. So after you have focused on the exercises you need to believe that everything you have aimed to do in this chapter will happen and let go of the end result. By awakening your intuition you are doing the opposite from the norm where you use willpower to attain success, as trying too hard to achieve results will be a turnoff to the higher mind. In the realm of the higher mind you don't need to force or push things to create success. The exercises are geared to allow magic to unfold and then you must allow it to do its job. If you want to understand more about trust review chapter three, page 83.

What we learn from a Primal Connection

It's time to reflect on all that you have discovered. You know that by becoming more aware of the balance of your energy and channelling your sexuality through tantric sex you can create a magical and powerful bond in your relationship. By raising your Kundalini you will not only develop a sensual and profound experience within your lovemaking but also heighten all your supernatural potential.

As a result you will feel more fulfilled on all levels, spiritually, emotionally and physically. Your relationship will be more balanced and honest as you retain the passion but also nurture an ongoing fire in your heart. Using your imagination, creativity and dreams will treble the impact, which will transform you and your partnership as your spirit takes the lead in all your decisions.

You no longer need to look back and wonder where that spark of passion went, get into power struggles or let lust drive your relationship. Follow the techniques and simply allow all your fine feelings of wisdom, compassion and empathy to come to the fore; persist in this new journey and your bond will naturally deepen.

You have read about the two quite different outcomes of couples who experienced a primal sexual connection. Despite this link being powerfully sexual you have seen how lust can still reap long-term rewards with a relationship that lasted the test of time. But you can also see how fragile this link can be when you get into a negative cycle of ongoing arguments and reconciliations that eventually burns itself out.

But by channelling your sexual energy through your imagination, dreams and tantric sex you can remain grounded and allow your relationship to evolve. It is too easy to remain stuck in old experiences that make you reactive. Clear out the ancient emotional issues that stagnate in your chakras and you will be able to create new patterns and respond to your partner with love and wisdom instead of just a physical longing.

Allow yourself to continue your adventure and experiment with other ways to develop your relationship, too. You may have discovered from the questionnaire in chapter three that you also have a mental rapport; if so turn to the exercises in chapter seven and learn how to use your psychic resources more fully. Then flick through the book and let your empowered intuition illuminate any exercises in the other chapters that will help you maximise your partnership potential. Go with whatever jumps out at you. This is an ongoing exploration that can only help you to build on what you already have.

Finally, remember to conclude our experience with the last chapter and see how far your journey of the heart has taken you.

7

THE MIND-TO-MIND CONNECTION

A RELATIONSHIP BUILT ON THE ELECTRIFYING AFFINITY OF A MENTAL RAPPORT

The mind is not a vessel to be filled but a fire to be kindled.

PLUTARCH, c. AD 46–c. 120, LEGENDARY PRIEST OF THE DELPHIC ORACLE

The quiz has highlighted your distinguishing link, the invigorating mental synergy of the mind-to-mind connection, the electrifying rapport that makes you feel as if you could talk for hours. You are fuelled and energised by each other's mind energy, which is addictive and inspiring.

In this connection, you will both click on an intellectual level where you have the same desire to learn about similar subjects, or have shared thoughts, ideas and understanding. Needless to say, this is the bond of friendship that often has real staying power in matters of the heart. Although you may have a healthy sex life, your connection isn't overly dominated by this fiery energy, and so you do not suffer from the problems that couples with a primal connection are prone to. Without the emotional and sexual forces bringing buried issues to the surface, you can enjoy developing this rapport at a steady pace.

Here you can learn more about this affinity and how to nurture the mind-to-mind link. They say sex starts in the mind and this type of energy leads to an arousal not only of passion but also of creativity and intellectual stimulation. At its fullest potential this flow leads to a synthesis between you as you know what the other is thinking even at a distance. Having learned about your relationship through the questionnaire you can use the four techniques to rekindle the rapport between you, breaking through any barriers or issues that have come between you.

By cleansing your mind of negative thoughts and beliefs and developing telepathic skills, you can focus your powerful mental force and use your psychic equipment, your imagination and creativity to transform yourself and your partner into awakened lovers with deep empathy, trust and love.

What is the mind-to-mind connection?

This connection is a shared intellectual rapport that fires you up on many levels. Many partnerships are formed on this bond alone and it is often the basis for long and stable relationships. The reason is that this link is usually based on friendship and a coming together of ideas, beliefs and interests, which means you are able to build a relationship gradually. Although you may be aware of a strong sexual attraction that you feel compelled to act on, you have the foundations of a strong rapport and understanding because of this shared meeting of minds. That is why the building blocks are often in place for continued relations with a feeling of trust and mutual respect that you may not get through pure blind passion. This creates a bedrock for a solid stabilising force that helps you overcome hurdles and difficulties that may present themselves. It also means that in the future, if the sexual interest wanes, it is still possible to retain the friendship that you began with.

Your mind rapport Partner

If you discovered that you have this type of affinity you will completely understand the term 'meeting of minds'. You probably wanted to talk for hours with your partner when you first met, as your strong mutual mind energy meant that you mirrored each other's ideas and thoughts. This energy may have fired up an instant feeling of sexual attraction or it may have linked you in a feeling of intellectual stimulation with a strong desire to know more about each other.

A mind-to-mind rapport doesn't mean there has to be a great intellectual link. But you will understand the way you both think, simply because you are on the same wavelength. Perhaps you met through some form of study, or even enjoyed learning together. You might agree with similar philosophies, beliefs or ideals, enjoy the same hobbies or have the same sense of humour. Many couples with this link have loving and successful marriages as they are always stimulated and interested by their mutual thoughts, which keep them fired up intellectually and sexually. Others who may not have such a strong sexual relationship still have a prosperous partnership because their comradeship is their unifying force and overrides any sexual disinterest. Fortunately, this means you have the ability to remain good supportive pals, able to retain your friendship long after a relationship has ended or any passion has waned.

A telepathic communication can flow easily between a couple on this wavelength as your mind energy merges together, but, like all the other attractions, whether there is a positive or negative outcome lies in how you handle your partnership.

Let's look at the following example and see how this couple overcame their personal hurdles to achieve an intuitive bond where they felt completely in tune with one another's needs and thoughts.

Charlotte's Story: achieving happiness

Charlotte, thirty-six, a health practitioner, met her partner Oliver forty-three, a livestock farmer, through mutual friends. She was in another relationship when they were introduced and they didn't get intimately involved with each other for eighteen months.

'There was no instant attraction or recognition,' says Charlotte. 'We had a shared rapport and I enjoyed his company but thought nothing more of him for a long time. But I always felt comfortable around Oliver as we could talk about our shared interests. We were both outdoorsy types very practical with no airs and graces and we both loved animals.

'We somehow continued seeing each other regularly once a week, by what I thought was just casually bumping into each other. He often used to pop into my friends' house when I was there, which he later confessed was deliberate. There was a flirty banter between us but nothing more.

'Over a year later when my relationship had come to an end, I helped him out with some farm work. It was a dark night but the stars seemed particularly bright that night and seemed to light up the sky. I remember Oliver stood behind me and put his hands on my shoulders and I suddenly felt his presence go through me as if we completely connected. It was from that moment on our friendship went to another stage and you couldn't separate us. It was like trying to pull two magnets apart. We spent nearly every day together and then a few weeks later, we finally admitted our feelings. One evening as we were sitting together on his settee he

looked at me tenderly and said, "I really love you." I didn't answer. I was so choked with emotion that I had to change the subject. It was a week later that I voiced my own mutual feelings.

'From then on we were an item in every sense and over the last few years he has been my greatest support. Things haven't always been plain sailing. I have suffered on and off with depression – which was due to delayed shock from a bereavement that happened a while back. When I'm feeling this way I find it hard to get out of bed, my sex drive takes a nosedive and I feel deeply melancholy and don't make much sense. But we always fall back on this amazing rapport that we have together. He'll always bring me up a cup of tea and ask me questions, trying to understand more about depression. He has even read up on the subject. Because of our mutual understanding and being able to talk about anything, we have overcome bad times and celebrated the good times. Even when we spend long periods of time together like on holiday we always have fun and never argue. We are both positive and look for the best in each other and, because of the strong friendship that we developed, we have an innate trust.

'Intuitively we are now very in sync with each other and that close mental affinity seems to have an extra bonus as we have both discovered that during the day we will quite naturally pick up on each other's thoughts telepathically. It's as if our minds are so in tune we can speak to each other without having to say too much. Sometimes I'll be rushing around and I'll think, God, I need some peace and quiet, and when I get back in the house, he's read my thoughts, dimmed the lights, put the bin out and fed the dog. And all I have to do is sit down with a glass of wine. We have an incredible rapport, but what's happened as we've grown closer is that we find we are just as content and comfortable when we are sitting in complete silence.'

This relationship proves that happy outcomes aren't always built on perfect circumstances. Despite Charlotte's depression they were able to communicate honestly and take time both to listen and understand each other. Charlotte realised it was important to explain to Oliver what was going on with her depression and he was able to discover more about the condition and empathise. He didn't take things personally when she lost her sex drive or felt lethargic, because their bond had been more than merely sexual for such a long time. They had a good foundation of shared interests and respect, and knew their feelings were more than surface deep. Their mutual telepathy stemmed from their strong mental bond, which grew to create empathy and compassion, and they supported each other without feeling compromised. Their positive attitude to look for the good in each other helped them to feel in tune.

Your mind-to-mind Potential

When your relationship works constructively, you will know what it is like to be best friends with your partner. You have a strong rapport and can be open and honest and talk about anything. This can also develop into a powerful affinity that can fire you up in other ways. Listening to your partner express views and ideas which you completely gel with is like balm to any negativity you may feel. As your inspired feelings plug you into your deeper intuitive powers you feel supported and it is also a passionate turn-on. There is nothing like a real meeting of minds to make you feel you want to connect in a sexual way.

If there is a problem with your physical relationship you are able to talk things through, as your mental affinity is the strongest force. Problems may arise if you stop communicating, because, unless you're one of the lucky ones, you don't have such a strong emotional and sexual dynamic to pull you through, so you must keep the lines of discussion open.

Your strong communication skills mean that you can quickly iron out differences or conflicts and share ideas that could be supportive to both of you.

It's time to look at your responses to the questionnaire in chapter three. Your answers to specific questions illuminate any detrimental weaknesses in your relationship. If you had more than one answer in the destructive category then there are serious problems in your relationship that need to be resolved. This is your chance to take an honest look at how you both relate.

Destructive Tendencies

If the questionnaire revealed destructive elements in your relationship then you can now focus on using your intuitive powers to nurture your positive feelings. The answers you have given have merely told you what you already knew deep down. Perhaps you are using that mental dexterity between you to hurl spiteful or condescending words at one another. You might feel you are debating over old ground endlessly without ever reaching any constructive outcomes. Equally, you might have stopped communicating altogether and be living a lie, yet simmer with repressed and resentful anguish. Do you want to relight the mind-to-mind fire between you or do you spend your time wishing you were with someone else? If you feel hostile, melancholy or unfulfilled within your partnership you know that things between you are not as they should be.

Instead of pushing issues to the back of your mind or putting on a brave face, you now know that you can transform your relationship – if you are willing. You can use your inherent psychic powers to refocus on that powerful mind-to-mind connection that drew you together. Eliminate your mind of mental junk – beliefs and attitudes that have piled up in your subconscious and are influencing the way you feel and behave. If left unresolved they will fester like a compost heap and make you feel depressed and irritable. Once you have used your psychic techniques to offload these you will be able to take the next step and tap in to your creativity and intuition to create loving psychic images of each other.

Feelings of Disconnection

The mind-to-mind partnership will feel a disconnection differently to relationships based on other links. You don't have the powerful emotional or sexual link to keep you nurtured in other ways. Given that a strong mental rapport is your fundamental link, if communication breaks down you could feel lonely and insular, as if you are strangers sharing the same home. If you allow negative feelings to build up and create barriers, then your partnership will suffer. Of course, many of you will relate well sexually and find ways of communicating through making love which keeps a stronger contact between you. But even if a sexual bond sustains you for a while, this cannot make up for discussing openly and honestly how you feel. As this is the spark that brought you together, nothing else will compensate for that close mental affinity.

Be honest and look at your partnership with an objective eye. Have you become like strangers? Are you going through the motions in your relationship, acting out your part but not communicating honestly? Are you bored, because you are not sharing any real connection? Do you feel uninterested in your partner or ignored by them? Do you push problems to the back of your mind instead of dealing with them?

Connecting with your intuition will help you to have honest communication that comes from your higher mind and not from your limited and negative thoughts and beliefs. Then you can find the way back to connect with your feelings of love. Once you talk, you can start to invest your own intuitive energy and communicate on more subtle levels.

But for some of you, it may be impossible to reconcile your differences and this is when you need to look at taking separate paths.

Knowing when it's time to move on

There are several signs that will alert you to the fact that you both need to move on. Firstly, if you both feel too uninterested to invest energy in your relationship then you won't achieve any results. It takes perseverance and enthusiasm to want to use the exercises in this book. Habitual patterns of conflict and non-communication can make it hard to change. If you have let things fester between you for too long or built up too many barriers, it may be too difficult to turn things around.

Secondly, it is typical of this type of connection that when problems arise you send a volley of words to each other in endless conflicts, trying to outsmart or patronise the other; you may well feel things have gone too far to put right. More than in any other connection, communication is the key here, and whether there is a lack of rapport or words fly aggressively, it will be harder for you to cope with. Rapport is your affinity and you don't have the emotional synergy and deep love of the soul mate connection or the ancient history of a past life to fuel you when things get tough. Nor can you use this intensity like the primal link and turn it into passion. So for you verbalising constructively how you feel is all-important.

Equally, if you want to see positive results, but your partner acts in a selfish, vindictive or distant way, then you have to face up to the stark reality that they may not ever be able to give you what you want. There is no point in deluding yourself or living a lie if you know your loved one cannot invest some love and commitment in the relationship. For a partnership to work it must be mutually giving and you both need to focus on the positive in each other and not dwell in the past or on problems. Aggression can also be expressed through actions and expressions, without words, which can be just as painful.

Only you know the truth and whether you have the courage to take another path in your life and find another love.

Understanding and Healing Your Mind-to-Mind Connection

If you are committed to your relationship then, rest assured, the exercises in this chapter will enable you to understand the way you connect on a mind level and help you to rekindle that mental affinity and allow it to take you to new heights. You can develop an incredible empathy and understanding as you learn to use specific exercises to draw you together. Reigniting the spark between you will fire up your mutual attraction as you become aware of the sensual and stimulating thrill of exploring the most potent organ – your mind.

You will go one step further this time and learn how to enjoy an adventure into your higher consciousness. By using your psychic powers to create new visions in your auric fields you can create a potent loving picture of what you ideally desire between you. You can send out erotic and loving thought forms and create a haven that is fuelled by abundant and positive thought forms. Anything is possible between you and in developing your psychic powers your mind powers will grow stronger as you strengthen a sense of telepathic empathy between you as your thoughts merge ever closer.

You are now at the first stage of the unique exercises that will channel and develop the higher aspects of your mind. Each exercise uses the second and third techniques of focusing your mind and employing your imagination in an evolving process. As you have such a strong thought connection with shared ideas and beliefs, an enormous amount of mental junk could be stored up if your relationship has soured. Unresolved problems, pressures and conflicts block your natural intuitive responses as you see everything through a warped perception.

So step one is designed to clear you of negative thoughts and beliefs, and once you have eliminated the junk that is disturbing your mind you can allow this positive resonance to flow between you again unhindered. You will then be ready to strengthen your psychic powers using your creativity and evoke a powerful sixth sense that can re-light the mind magic between you. The results are transformational. Your communication will be more honest and open as you feel you can speak from your heart and you will gain an intuitive understanding of each other. You will feel calmer and more balanced and see each other clearly rather than responding with knee-jerk reactions. And through the power of thought transference you can ignite the bed-sheets by influencing your partner with passionate thoughts and learn real intimacy by sensing how they feel and think even from a distance. You are instrumental in the way your relationship flourishes and you can use your own magical powers to create a supernatural bond with unconditional love and a profound intimacy.

Free your mind

This first exercise uses your imaginative skills to cleanse your mind of unwanted problems and issues that are holding you and your partner back. By freeing yourself of old issues that colour your perception and reactions you cleanse your energy field, so that you can create a positive vision that isn't clouded by negative feelings. If we allow old emotions to fester, whether from our childhood, or past and present relationships, they create interference in our perception of our current relationship and of the world. This technique will allow you to access your higher mind and liberate yourself from your old thought energy. You are then ready to create new positive beliefs and thought forms, which will synchronise you with a higher vibrational frequency that will help you see your partnership clearly and inject supernatural magic into your love life with a fresh perspective.

Find somewhere quiet to sit and if you wish play some soft melodic music to get you in the mood and block out background noise. Before you begin your imaginative journey think about all the obstacles and conflicts that are influencing your relationship. Then visualise yourself and your partner in a woodland setting on a spring afternoon. There are many varieties of trees around you with lush greenery and you can smell the scent of wild flowers that grow beside a long winding path. You can hear the crunch of twigs and leaves as you stroll along. As you walk you can hear the sounds of nature: the rustling of leaves and branches and in the distance birds are singing.

Not far off you see some wooden steps that ascend to an ornate

Japanese bridge. You head towards it to take a closer look. You are both drawn to walk up the steps and you do so slowly, feeling the smooth surface, partly covered in ivy and leaves, beneath your feet. There is a wooden banister to hold on to and you notice how it is entwined with jasmine and roses. Walk up each step for as long as it takes to get there and as you do so feel all the old conflicts and problems gently rising to the surface of your mind. When you reach the bridge you see a stunning view as you find you are looking over a large clear pool where numerous water lilies float on the surface and it is edged by a weeping willow and several large apple trees. As the apple blossom falls off the trees, you can smell its delicate fragrance pervading the air.

Visualise yourself standing next to your partner and feel all your negative issues and thoughts rising to the top of your head. Note that the same is happening with your partner. Take time to focus on yourself first and visualise that the top of your head has opened and that you are going to let all your negative thoughts and feelings free. Imagine all your conflicts and misunderstandings have wings and the instant the top of your head opens they fly out. You don't have to see them specifically but sense your thoughts as energies flying away into the sky towards the sun. Allow this to continue for as long as you need, as many thoughts arise from your stomach, shoulders or legs – any place where you feel you hold tension and anxiety. As you imagine them leaving your head, your mind feels lighter and clearer.

When you have completely finished visualise the same thing happening with your partner. Don't worry about what happens to these negative forms of energy. As soon as they get close to the sun they will be neutralised and become part of the solar energy. Now visualise the golden rays of the sun pouring over you and the radiant light cleansing and filling you up; again see the same thing happening to your partner.

When you are ready take a deep breath and slowly make your way back down the wooden steps to the forest with your partner following. Feel yourself become more grounded and alert as you are back in the woodland setting. Now become conscious of where you are in the room you are relaxing in.

The After-Effects

This exercise was an important first step. You have cleared away a lot of old energies from your auric field, which will make you less stressed, and exercised your higher mind so that you can begin to feel more receptive towards your partner. It is important to free your mind from these types of thoughts and feelings so that you can see each other objectively and feel more balanced within yourselves. How do you feel now? Do you get a sense of light-headedness or having more clarity? Perhaps you feel more relaxed and open. If you're not aware of any difference, don't worry; the effects of your intent will none the less have a strong influence and you will have cleared away some of the mental debris from both your and your partner's auric fields. You may experience emotional feelings that you have been suppressing, but this is a good thing as the more we connect with how we feel, the more we release it and move on. Otherwise our appreciation of our present circumstances is hampered by past thoughts. We can overreact to our partner or events in our lives because of these old issues. Simply allow yourself to feel whatever it is and let it go. Don't stew on it. Just acknowledge the feelings and say mentally, 'I accept this feeling,' and then experience it.

Ask your partner how they felt at the time you did the exercise. They might have felt a sudden calming impact wherever they were. Thoughts and intention are powerful. This exercise ensured that you both feel more open and relaxed with each other and eased any tension or conflict that had arisen between you. In turn this will help you to connect with your partner without old conflicts creating barriers. Having released dammed-up energy, it will also help you to activate your psychic muscle, as your mind energy expands with the use of your imagination. You can use this exercise any time you want to clear away old issues that are affecting your relationship, and thereby feel freer, more energised and optimistic within yourself.

Now you have cleared your mind you will see how crucial this exercise was for your relationship. To illustrate what happens if you don't take the time to do this, read what happened when a couple with a strong mind-to-mind connection allowed negative thought energies in the form of work issues and insecurity to create a detrimental influence on their relationship.

Linda's story: the negative cycle

Linda, a twenty-six-year-old dancer, met her estate agent partner Bob, thirty-six when she was buying a house six years ago. 'There was a strong rapport from the start and we shared the same sense of humour and interests' says Linda.

'We discovered we'd had a very similar history in relationships and that seemed to create a mutual understanding. He then asked me away for a weekend. We talked into the early hours and it felt like I'd really met someone who understood the way I see things.

'For the first six months it was idyllic. It was as if I'd found a best friend and we quickly moved in together. But six years later, that great spark hasn't stopped our relationship becoming an emotional rollercoaster ride. When we got on well, we could talk about anything and feel as if we really gelled. Our sex life was good and we had fun together. But when things were bad, I felt very isolated as if we were more like flatmates living separate

lives. He'd go out with his friends after work and I'd go out with mine and our paths fleetingly crossed in the hallway. Either we didn't speak at all or I'd suddenly lash out at him. We've both ended up saying some very spiteful things to each other. This proved really hard for me as our ability to communicate was the strongest connection that we had. Without it I felt lost.

'The main problems have been triggered through a lack of quality time due to Rob building up his estate agency business. As a consequence we didn't get a chance to talk and he was always stressed and tired. I'd end up wondering what was going on in his life and whether I'd ever be part of it. He was in work mode so much of the time he seemed to find it hard to switch on to our personal life.

'The past also affected me. My previous partner had left me for another woman and Bob had admitted being unfaithful to his last girlfriend. When I felt he wasn't around to give me attention I would suddenly start an argument and scream at him hysterically and that would make him instantly disappear out of the house.

'Because of this, at times it's been a turbulent minefield with constant threats of breaking up, and me feeling upset and miserable.

'However, there are still times when I feel haunted by the fact that he might leave me and I wish I could feel calmer within myself so I don't keep lashing out in anger. I often wish I had a magical formula to overcome these barriers. I really want to make our relationship work and if we continue the way we are it will feel more like a prison sentence than a relationship. It is depressing to think we live like this when we had such an incredible rapport when we first met.'

As we all know only too well, however great the spark in our relationship there are always going to be times for the most loving of couples when there are conflicts, misunderstandings, stress or seething undercurrents. This couple's story reveals how difficult it can be when outside pressures come between you and cause conflicts and you have insecurity from the past. This is the time when telepathic thought transference can build your bridges and soothe any angst. Tuning in to your higher mind also enables you to connect with a calming vibration that makes you feel more balanced. You are therefore not so prone to attack your partner but are able to relate in a more understanding way.

Despite their current difficult circumstances, Linda and Bob could have made up for any lack of intimacy when they did spend time together. By using intuitive exercises they could have maintained a strong loving connection even from a distance.

If Linda had used her psychic powers to transform her relationship, Bob would have experienced loving thoughts flashing through his mind. He would have felt like making more telephone calls to Linda because of the warm feelings that were being evoked. He would have been prompted to cut short his socialising and come home earlier because he felt such an unconscious pull towards Linda. Then when they did spend time together they would have had a natural affinity of warmth and tenderness without any barriers.

Dissolving barriers with psychic energy

Never underestimate the power of a single thought, especially those that are fuelled with strong emotions such as hate, love, jealousy and passion. The invisible force of thoughts will make the recipient feel a sudden surge of warmth and affection towards you or feel a sense of irritation, depression or anger. Fleeting thoughts have little effect and merely drift through us.

So if you've had an argument with your partner, instead of brooding silently, which will send out more poisonous energy, decide consciously to send out powerful loving thoughts.

This is an incredibly beneficial way to heal a rift, inject passion into a stale relationship and soothe communications in all our relationships. Your partner will feel the subtle effects of your positive thought energy as they suddenly get a sense of you filtering through their mind and feel uplift, excitement or tenderness, and they won't be able to help but think of you warmly. Remember repetition and intention is the key. The power of your mind is such that your partner will respond quite unconsciously to the energy that you send out to them.

Using creativity to tune in to your partner

The next exercise will help you to activate your intuitive powers by developing your creativity. Creativity stems from the same source as your sixth sense, which is governed by the right side of your mind (see chapter three, page 74). It is essential to stimulate this part of your mind so that you develop it and heighten your intuition. This artistic aspect can be used as a channel to gain more awareness and insight into your partnership. The more you generate this inspired thought, the more you will expedite your psychic powers and feel more aware, receptive and in tune with your partner.

Creativity is an important ingredient for a deeper relationship bond. As your connection sparks off communication on many levels between you, focus on inspired ideas. The more you see your creative ideas become reality in any form, the more you will strengthen the seventh level of your aura. Using it in your relationship means that you heighten your vibrational frequency, which plugs you into your feelings of love, empathy and compassion. Two people who develop this aspect of their higher mind can experience a strong sixth sense where they telepathically know what the other is thinking. This will give you a deep understanding of your partner's needs and a sense of magical closeness. It will help you to achieve the ultimate aim, even for short periods, of a sense of complete oneness and unity as you feel your mind energy merge.

This is the next step to help you achieve that aim. You both already have a head start, as your mental energy was already in sync. Although you can be creative in any area of your life, whether cooking, gardening, or hobbies such as painting or sculpting, this exercise is perfect for the kind of mind energy you both have, as you will soon discover.

Creative writing

This way of writing will enable you to focus your mind so that your higher mind can filter through inspired information. The subject of this exercise is your own love story. Not only will you develop the right, intuitive side of your mind and tap in to your psychic voice but you will also focus on the positive elements of your relationship and the spark that first brought you together. This will remind you why you are together and how important it is to relight that spark and bring intuition back into your life, instead of allowing stress and conflicts to colour your reactions.

Don't analyse what you write: What matters is that the information helps you to gain understanding and insight into the nature of your relationship. How did you both meet? Bring the scenario to life and elaborate on the scene as if you are watching a movie in your head. Try to focus on the emotions you both felt and remember how you looked at each other. Your talents in this area are immaterial. Simply see this as an exercise to build a bridge to your higher mind and help yourself recall the spark.

The exercise will be more effective if you take turns to relive your meeting. And it will be interesting to see how you each perceive events. But you can reap the benefit even if your partner is not present. Refocusing on the positive feelings between you by going back into the past will unconsciously affect your loved one. It is a reminder of how things have moved on but also why you were affected by that initial attraction. Unlocking the door to your intuitive and creative self will enable you to release any unresolved issues and strengthen your bond. Relating from this higher part of yourself creates more positive, loving responses between you both as you assimilate your experiences and become more of who you really are.

Your Creative Love Story

Find a peaceful environment where you won't be disturbed. Either use a notepad and pen or sit in front of your computer. Allow your mind to wander back to your courtship. How did you meet and where was it? What was your first sense of meeting your partner? Was there an instant spark of attraction or was it a friendship that built up over time? What was it about your partner that you found so attractive? How did the affinity between you affect you? Did you feel a sense of kinship and trust? Did you talk all night? Were there hurdles to overcome that finally brought you together? How precious was this relationship to you?

All these elements are part of your treasured love story. It was the moment that your paths crossed and what transpired from that meeting. Write your love story and by bringing it back into your mind's eye, you relive the energy from that time. It is this initial awakening of attraction that you want to evoke in your relationship but in a stronger and deeper way. As your creativity flows, it may trigger old memories and romantic scenarios that you had long forgotten.

It is important that you see clearly the journey that your partnership has taken, and the attraction that first brought you together. On an energy level you have focused on how things were and created a vision of what you want to achieve, only bigger and better. This will send out vibrations towards your partner and evoke memories of the emotional responses that were triggered in you both. This exercise is a powerful blueprint for bringing back from the past what you want to create for the future, but this time you have an opportunity to turn that spark into flames. You may find that you have more lucid insights into your relationship as you have expressed your emotions and tuned in to who you both are in essence and not how you react to events.

You have reached an important stage in this chapter where you can transform yourselves into the supernatural lovers you aspire to be. It was necessary initially to do the groundwork to exercise your intuition and allow your mind to be free to create psychic images. Whatever your circumstances, whether bored, angry, insecure or feeling abandoned, you can use this next telepathy exercise to turn your relationship into a loving, secure bond with a magical formula to help you handle any obstacle that may arise. The more you inject warm waves of energy into your relationship, the more you will receive.

Strengthening your connection through telepathy

By focusing your mind in this exercise you will be able to develop telepathic communication between you. This has a remarkable twofold effect. Not only will you become more receptive to picking up your lover's thoughts but you can also create a positive and loving influence that will penetrate your partner's mind and they will suddenly feel a surge of warmth towards you. Their thoughts about you, regardless of previous conflicts, will be inspired, loving and open. The more you create this loving influence, the more intimacy, trust and love you will engender between you. As a result not only will they want to spend more time with you, but when you do see each other there will be a strong affinity between you, and your reality will start to mirror your vision in feelings and outcome. This involves using your imagination, which will expand your mind energy and release stress as well as heighten all your intuitive and creative powers.

Instead of focusing on any failings or annoyances about your partner and your relationship, you are now operating from an inner vision of success. Your new expectations, heightened intuition and energised aura charged with loving thoughts and beliefs will send out magnetic vibes to create a powerfully loving intimacy and trust within your relationship.

By continually building up this energy, you will open up a channel for telepathy between you. You may sense when your partner is thinking of you. A picture of them may flash through your mind, or you may get a surge of warmth or a strong feeling of closeness. The more you practise the exercise the closer you will become. If your partner wishes, they can do the same with you and soon you can open up a stronger telepathic channel where you can project thoughts or feelings at your whim. Your relationship can take on many dimensions using this powerful technique. You will feel a profound intimacy and sense of security as you develop skills that will enable you to influence and connect with your partner's mind wherever they are in the world. You will feel that you are part of a special union, as you can influence them with emotion, passion or ask a simple question and receive a response. The mind is an incredible energy force and by directing it in the way you want, your partnership will flourish dramatically.

Positive thoughts are good for you too. Uplifting visions keep your mind energy expanding outwards, heightening your intuition and giving you a sense of expectancy and optimism.

Tune into telepathy thought transference and create the love life of your dreams

Think of how you would like your relationship to be. Conjure up a scene in your mind that sums up your ideal. Focus on intimacy and affection. Rewind to one of the most romantic loving times you shared together. How did you feel? Was there a sense of adrenaline? Did you feel loving and tender towards your partner? Was there an electric passion between you and a magical affinity? Remember how wonderful you felt your partner was and the qualities that attracted you and how you brought out the best in each other. Despite any hostility or indifference that you may have felt towards your partner of late, recreate that positive emotion all over again.

Now you have evoked old feelings, visualise a scene gazing into your partner's eyes; sense how you are both feeling. Feel the intimacy and the love that exist between you. Feel that bond and visualise the energy flowing between your heart chakras (see chapter four on soul mates and chakra exercise).

Next visualise a more detailed scene that you both enjoy and make it your perfect present reality. It might be an intimate candlelit dinner, a cosy fireside chat or making love. Imagine the scenario and ensure the picture is loaded with all your sensory feelings. If you are having a fireside chat, visualise the warmth from the flames on your skin, focus on what you are both wearing; choose an outfit that your partner really likes and you feel comfortable in. How does the carpet or rug you are sitting on feel? Perhaps your favourite CD is playing in the background and you are drinking some wine, or maybe a cup of hot coffee. How does it taste? What is the lighting like in the room? Is it subtle candle-light or is there just a glow from the fire illuminating your faces?

See the vision as it is happening now and picture your own front room rather than an imaginary one to give added power to your images. This isn't a made-up fantasy but a mind creation that will affect your reality. Remember to send out all this energy with trust and not a needy response. Don't anticipate how they will react, just visualise and then let go of the outcome, otherwise they will pick up your neediness as a form of control and it will change the positive effects. With so much loving energy bombarding them, how could they fail to respond?

With this technique you are doing all the romantic preparation when you are apart, even on a working day, before you enjoy some quality time together. Even if you don't normally manage to spend much time with one another, you may be amazed at how quickly your partner suggests a romantic dinner, or a reshuffle of their schedule as you are in the forefront of their thoughts. Trust your psychic powers and get ready to turn up the heat on your relationship all over again.

Send a telepathic sex bomb

If you want to evoke passion in your relationship you can send sensual mind pictures to raise your lover's temperature. Imagine making love as realistically as possible. If it's in your bedroom, concentrate on all your senses and whether there is music playing in the background. Make the imaginative atmosphere erotically charged and get a sense of heightened arousal.

If you want to make it more emotional and tender then send energy from your heart chakra, or if you want them simply to feel sexy send it from your second splenic chakra and keep projecting the potent image. They will soon receive a surge of buzzing sensual energy which will remind them of your presence and get them in the mood for love.

If you want to know more about stimulating sexual energy in your relationship you can learn more about tantric sex in chapter six, page 204.

Increasing the result through affirmations

Affirmations are repeated statements which double the power of a visualisation when they complement what you see in your mind's eye. The combination of a visualisation and an affirmation has powerful results in creating the vision of what you want to achieve. They focus and empower your thoughts, convincing your subconscious mind that you mean business. Affirmations that complement your vision can be something like, 'We are happy and secure together,' 'We feel loving and passionate towards each other.' 'Love and happiness are flowing between us.'

We say and visualise things in the present because the mind doesn't understand the past or future. It only experiences what is happening in the now. Visualising your relationship positively, as if it is already happening, creates an experience of that reality in your body and emotions recharging your auric field. Your vision is sent out to your partner as if you are already enjoying that loving intimacy. They will quite unconsciously sense a strong feeling of warmth and pick up the message that you are having dinner together, making love or whatever else you imagined. They will suggest meeting up in the way that you visualised or respond very well if you make a suggestion.

Take note: this visualisation exercise can achieve powerful results to help expand your higher minds and allow your intuitive selves to open up and make you feel even more in sync. It will be more effective if your partner joins you by using their imagination at the same time as you, so you can explore this journey together. But if they are reluctant or simply too busy, you can still build a closer intuitive rapport by visualising them in a loving scenario.

Questions to ask yourself

1. How did you feel about visualising? Was it difficult to get a clear picture or create loving feelings? If you find it hard, you may not have a well-honed visual sense but keep practising to get a sense of the scenario, how you feel and where you are sitting. Then imagine you both together sharing affection. The more mental dexterity you develop to enliven all your senses, the more your mind will expand, heightening your psychic powers, and the more your partner will be influenced. Do whatever you can to begin with and you will still make progress in recreating the passion and love you want to achieve.
2. How are you managing to mix the affirmations with your visualisation? If you find it difficult to hold a vision and make a mental statement at the same time, persevere, see the picture in your mind and then repeat the

affirmation. It will take practice and initially you may wish to do them separately until you get into the habit.

Choose your Telepathic Time Zone

After you have begun to visualise, you can empower your telepathy technique by a very simple exercise. Before you embark on any telepathy, choose a time every day when you have the opportunity to be relaxed and your partner is obviously absent. It could be just fifteen to thirty minutes when you could visualise and send out positive thoughts to your partner. Whatever time you can spare. The reason for picking a time slot is that the mind responds well to habitual patterns. For example, something like learning to drive or type can be a skill that you have to concentrate hard on at first, but with practice you learn to do it automatically. By keeping to the same hour, your mind will gradually focus more readily, and unconsciously anticipate that time for positive thinking. As you continue, this specified period will become very powerful and healing and when you are either together or apart you will automatically send out positive energy and create a surge of warm feelings.

Your partner will be affected by your positive influence whether they know you are doing it or not. You could even have two time periods every day. This block of time will become a sacred force of energy, when you stimulate the already powerful energy that runs between both your minds. When you do spend time together you will have heightened energy around this time period. You can use your healing time to discuss any problems or issues that might arise between you and the energy will help you to remain harmonised and constructive.

Trust

You have now discovered many ways to unleash your higher self and allow your mind to focus on developing your relationship. You are in an awakened partnership where you can nurture each other on an energy level and see the physical results manifest. To implement the full technique of trust, for these exercises to take effect you need to have faith that they will work and that involves remaining positive and letting go of the outcome. Controlling or dwelling on whether something will work is an aspect of your limited mind, not of someone who is connected with their inner voice. Focus on the psychic exercise and what you want to resolve and then let it go, knowing that loving energy will flow regardless of the conflicts between you. In a moment you can reawaken the pure and boundless vibration of unconditional love and find a new way of communicating that brings out the best in both of you.

Next discover what you can learn from a mind-to-mind connection that can enable you to harness the mind synergy between you and give yourselves a heightened understanding.

What we learn from a mind-to-mind connection

The case studies in this chapter reveal how you can create positive or negative outcomes in your relationships. The more you stay connected to your intuitive self and allow your finer qualities to guide you, the more beneficial your communication and the more constructive the outcome.

If you allow yourself to respond to your partner from your ego and limited mind, you will easily fall into playing complex mind games that lead to misery and isolation. Bear in mind that the expression 'mind games' is not usually about deliberately upsetting a partner, but more to do with unconscious reactions from the past that haven't been resolved. Our minds are creatures of habit and once we are used to reacting with criticism, negativity and intolerance it can be hard to break the cycle. When you are both in this state of mind, you simply set up a domino effect of responses that lead to barriers and defensive behaviour.

That's why it is so crucial to step out of this playing field and move into the expansive energy of your higher mind. You have much to gain, as with this type of rapport you have a powerful mental synergy that simply needs to be fine-tuned for you to amplify that incredible resonance between you.

Keep the Learning curve

Continue with the learning you take from your relationship, which will help you to understand its immense value.

- Keep up with your diary so that you can see how your relationship has blossomed since the beginning of the book.
- Remind yourself of any links in coincidences and insights that happen in your life. Once you write these down you will be surprised at the outcome of events or the way in which your relationship has developed.
- Note times when you have a problem or communication difficulties and don't fall into the pattern of giving knee-jerk reactions. Use the intuitive exercises and see your partner's response. There needs to be clarity on both sides for things to be remedied on a long-term basis and a re-education of thought processes. Mutually disciplining your mind to think constructively is crucial not only to the success of a relationship but also to the expansion of your higher consciousness.
- Be persistent if you want to make a breakthrough. The more

willing you are to work on your relationship, the more permanent and positive the effects. A perpetually negative state of mind is an isolating trap, but insight into ourselves and taking responsibility for thoughts stem from a place of balance.

Remember that however bad your relationship has become, even if you have reached a stalemate miracles can happen, but not always overnight. Give it time for the passion and love to be injected back into your partnership and your mind-to-mind spark to be reignited. This is one area in your life where the effort is not only enhancing your natural psychic powers but also creating a loving legacy that will have a healing effect on you and your family.

Reflect on how you have developed your intuition and begun to transform your relationship. You have discovered how to rid yourself of negative thoughts, using your imaginative powers to clear out the clutter in your mind that was distorting your perspective.

Your creativity will also help you to connect with your psychic self and enable your insights and inspiration to come to the fore. You have gone back into the past to bring those memories into the present and create a vision of how you want to feel once again. You have also learned the techniques of telepathic communication between you and your partner and the profound effects the power of a single thought can have when charged with positive, loving emotion. Not only will you be able to use your thoughts to change a mood or create a loving scenario, but this will bring an intimacy that will mean you can express your feelings from any distance. The closer bond you have forged will have a knock-on effect in all areas of your relationship, helping you to feel more connected sexually, emotionally and spiritually.

An additional benefit of using your mind in this way will be a flourishing relationship with yourself as well as with your mind-to-mind lover. Your insights will grow as you develop more harmony in all aspects towards your partner and problems can be a thing of the past, as you know how to inject positive loving energy into any conflict to turn things around.

Be sure to use this book intuitively. As you flick through the soul mate, past life and primal chapters, ask yourself what other exercises would be useful to you. You may have different needs at different times that another psychic activity can fulfil. Go with what feels right for you; you are on an evolving journey so keep developing your intuitive powers in many creative ways to strengthen your bond. Your imagination is the bridge that will give you true insight into the alchemy of your consciousness.

Enjoy your journey into unconditional love and the status of being the ultimate supernatural lover. Your time is now.

8 THE MAGICAL RECIPE FOR A LOVE LESS ORDINARY

YOUR VOYAGE INTO AN UNLIMITED FUTURE

Love has no other desire but to fulfil itself
But if you love and must needs have desires, let these be your desires:
To wake at dawn with a winged heart and give thanks for another day of loving;
And then to sleep with a prayer for the beloved in your heart
and a song of praise upon your lips.

KAHIL GIBRAN, 1883–1931, PHILOSOPHER AND PROPHET

Well done! You have achieved an enormous milestone in discovering some valuable tools on your eventful odyssey into intuitive love. As soon as you opened the pages of this book, whether you realised it or not, something deep within you wanted to revolutionise your love life. And as you set about using the psychic techniques something remarkable happened: everything changed and you set out on an inner quest to enter a new dimension and a different way of relating.

You and your partner are now intrepid explorers travelling to a new and exciting destination in unchartered territory, where the language spoken is the intuitive voice of the heart. In this place you will learn how to feel and enjoy profound intimacy, understanding and unconditional love. With your psychic self in the driving seat, you have taken off into new heights, and are travelling towards your higher partnership destiny; the outcome can only be a glorious adventure as you become the pioneer of a new way of living and loving in your relationship. Some of you may already have found it. You will know if you have, because you will feel that you are already home.

You can focus your mind and use your dreams, imagination and creativity to support your relationship. You can experience a real union with your partner as you harness your higher mind and create telepathy and empathy. Whatever your connection you can learn to bond in many other ways: mentally, spiritually, emotionally and sexually. The more you allow your energy to flow and rid yourself of old fears and beliefs, the more fully you connect with your partner.

So say goodbye to your old existence. You are no longer robotically living a stale life and pretending to be happy. You have taken off the mask and pledged to allow the intuitive voice of your spirit to come to the fore. Don't stop now! You have an opportunity to live and love in a way that you may not have previously thought possible. Whatever relationship problems, conflicts or issues you had are now in the past. You are not looking at what you have to accept, but what you can transform. That doesn't mean that problems will disappear. Your partner may still press your buttons and circumstances may prove challenging, but now you have the tools to change things. You are not a victim but a creator of your life ready to experience unconditional love with a fire in your heart and a passion for creating an extraordinary connection with your chosen companion. Let me congratulate you. It took courage to defy convention and take a new path. It takes courage to renew your belief in love and trust that miracles can happen.

As you put this book to one side don't underestimate the power of this moment. You have taken responsibility for the way you think and feel, therefore empowering yourself as a psychic being in charge of your own mind and life, rather than believing that you are a victim of fate destined to be unlucky in love.

From now on you have the magical tools to transform your relationship into an exciting, loving union where you can explore the higher mysteries of your mind to develop a new way of relating.

The golden guidelines for Higher Love

Having come this far, you need to keep developing your higher mind and your relationship. Don't worry about becoming an expert. It is more important that you remain a student of higher love. The more you allow your intuition to guide you, the more your relationship will blossom. But bear in mind that it's all too easy to slip back into our old limited ways, governed by negativity, insecurity and fear. So I have laid out some golden guidelines that will help you to keep that fire in your heart burning brightly.

Create a haven for love

Turn your bedroom into a peaceful, sensual room that will inspire the workings of your higher mind and evoke feelings of serenity and passion. Treat this room as a sacred place where love is the driving force. You want to ensure a feeling of harmony and uplift when you walk into the room. This is your launch pad for passion, a place where you can rise above the mundane and share in the deeper essence of each other.

- Always ensure your bedroom is clean and free from clutter. Untidiness affects us unconsciously and makes us feel irritable. Give the walls a fresh coat of paint and decorate it with warm sensual orange, or terracotta which will stimulate your second splenic chakra which feeds our vitality and sexuality. Pink is a colour that inspires love and there are shades like fuchsia or even a reddish pink that are inspirational and help open up the heart chakra. Green also governs the heart and emerald or jade harmonise and create balance.
- Hang inspiring pictures on the wall that evoke romance and passion. Art and other forms of creativity inspire our higher selves and raise our vibration.
- Focus on your bedding and make sure it is comfortable but attractive. You want your bed to be a place that you can't wait to climb into. Arrange scatter cushions in lush satin and velvet over the top and cover the duvet or sheets with a beautiful spread.
- Place scented candles around the room on tables, windowsills and shelves, but make sure they are safe. Or use light incense or scented oil to create a pleasant aroma. Display a vase of flowers; you can always have silk flowers instead of the real thing to give a splash of colour.
- Have a focal point like a statue that represents romance, such as Eros or Diana, goddess of love. It will serve as a reminder of what this atmosphere represents. Anything that reminds us mentally of our goals will keep inspiring us.
- Play some music in your bedroom. A favourite melody can soothe you and create a wonderful mood and also block out annoying background noise.

- Remove computers and televisions from the bedroom. These give off currents of electricity that interfere with your vibration and can stop you relaxing. They are also a distraction and in your new modus operandi you are creating intimacy, not focal points that turn you away from each other.
- Leave all rows and sulking outside the bedroom door. Hostile energy will effect the vibration of this room. Inject the room with loving higher thought frequencies by meditating and practising your visualisations in here.
- Keep pets out of your bedroom. This is a focused place for you and your partner, not extra-curricular guests.
- As soon as you feel your child is old enough, ensure that they have their own room. It is important in establishing their own independence and identity to have a room that is theirs alone.
- Make time for each other. Both you and your partner need focused intimate time and a room that will evoke this.

Be positive

Whatever challenge you have faced with your partner, however many times you have seen each other's darker side, experienced conflicts, sulked, felt self-pity, loathing or anger towards them, know that there is an inner spirit that is striving to transform. Instead of believing that your partner sees the worst in you, or even more commonly that you see the worst in yourself, believe that deep down they are conspiring to provide you with valuable lessons and an opportunity to experience unconditional love. This is quite different from an all-consuming love, which is an obsessional state that rules out everything but the chosen object of desire. Unconditional love is the intuitive vibration that equals acceptance, appreciation and giving without any trade-off. So congratulations: this is where your life really begins. It is your curtain call, your chance to rearrange the scenery in your mind and create the love life of your dreams.

Be Persistent

Be persistent. Practise the exercises to develop your higher mind and send your partner focused loving energy. Don't give up at the first hurdle. Just because your partner snaps at you, or is sullen or quiet, don't dismiss the intuitive work that you have done. Nobody is perfect and, despite any psychic exercises, if you or your partner is tired, hungry, hormonal or stressed they will not be able to respond with clarity. When situations like this occur, remember we are all human and give generously by offering a massage, run them a warm bath or invite your partner into the haven you have created. As soon as they relax your loving energy will begin to filter through. Bear in mind, too, that they may not always be up for an intensive work-out in the bedroom. They might just want some space or a good sleep, which is why it's essential to make quality time for each other if you want your partnership to blossom.

Trust

I cannot over-emphasise how trust is imperative. Without it you will not attain the results you want. Trust means you allow things to flow. It is a response from your higher mind. When you don't trust in the outcome or your vision of the relationship you want, you are coming from your limited mind and a place of ego and control. You have to trust that your psychic exercises will do their work and that your partner will respond. And you have to trust that you have the power to reignite the spark between you and create the powerful synergy you both deserve. Focus your mind on the exercises and dreams to create unconditional love and empathy and let go of your expectations and any outcome. Surrender to your vision and trust absolutely that it will work. What have you got to lose?

Enjoy Yourself

Keep a sense of humour. That means relax and enjoy the process. Developing your sixth sense and transforming your relationship can sound like serious business, but in the world of intuition you need to do the opposite from the norm. Trying too hard to achieve results will be a turnoff to your higher mind and to your partner. Becoming an awakened supernatural lover is not an exam that you need to pass, or a road with a destination at the end. There is no absolute finish line. It is a gradual unfolding of heightened awareness and unconditional love, like a flower that opens and the perfume fills the air. So have fun. Stay focused with intent on what you want, but surrender your expectations. This is about exploration and experimentation. That way you will leave room for anything to happen and your supernatural magic can begin to do its work.

A final note

When people first fall in love, they often describe feeling excited but scared, that there was a bigger force than they had known. It is, after all, a risky business to open your heart and simply feel. Love is not usually convenient or expected. When we meet someone with whom we connect and there is a huge force of energy, it rocks our world as we know it. Suddenly our comfortable rut has shifted and we are put in touch with a greater energy within. It moves our life force and pushes us to wake up. It unbalances us because we know there is a force more powerful than our will, but yet we can't see it or rationalise it. It forces us to be vulnerable and to be humbled by a power bigger than our egos. Yes, love is a transformational business. So do you give in to the fear and run away, or do you allow yourself to be part of an unlimited adventure and wake up to who you really are?

In case you thought otherwise, reading this book was no accident. Your sixth sense brought you here to show you that your psychic power to create the relationship you want is immense. The way forward is simple and easy if we allow it to be. We simply have to let go of our ideas of how to attain happiness and trust our inner voice to lead us to our goals. You have come a long way on this expedition into your higher mind and if you are ready to keep learning and loving, be prepared for a continuing transformation process. You have a golden future in a supernatural magical relationship with a chemistry that fizzles and a spark of fiery passion that can only explode into enduring flames.

Keep tuned in

If you're interested in being informed of any new books, seminars, or tapes coming out then you can stay connected via my website: Sherronmayes.com or Sherronmayes.co.uk. Equally, use this website to share your success stories or give your review of the book.

INDEX

Figures in italics indicate a caption.

INDEX

INDEX

INDEX